USDA

United States
Department of
Agriculture

Forest Service

Pacific Northwest
Research Station

General Technical Report
PNW-GTR-752
July 2008

Assessment of Timber Availability From Forest Restoration Within the Blue Mountains of Oregon

Technical Editors

Robert Rainville, now retired, was a Forest Service ranger and director of the Blue Mountains Demonstration Area, headquartered in La Grande, OR. **Rachel White** is a science writer and **Jamie Barbour** is a research forest products technologist, U.S. Department of Agriculture, Forest Service, Pacific Northwest Research Station, Forestry Sciences Laboratory, 620 SW Main St., Suite 400, Portland, OR 97205.

Cover photo by Mark Reid.

Assessment of Timber Availability From Forest Restoration Within the Blue Mountains of Oregon

Robert Rainville, Rachel White, and Jamie Barbour,
Technical Editors

U.S. Department of Agriculture
Forest Service
Pacific Northwest Research Station
Portland, OR
General Technical Report PNW-GTR-752

July 2008

Abstract

Rainville, Robert; White, Rachel; Barbour, Jamie, tech. eds. 2008. Assessment of timber availability from forest restoration within the Blue Mountains of Oregon. Gen. Tech. Rep. PNW-GTR-752. Portland, OR: U.S. Department of Agriculture, Forest Service, Pacific Northwest Research Station. 65 p.

Changes in forest management have detrimentally affected the economic health of small communities in the Blue Mountain region of Oregon over the past few decades. A build-up of small trees threatens the ecological health of these forests and increases wildland fire hazard. Hoping to boost their economies and also restore these forests, local leaders are interested in the economic value of timber that might be available from thinning treatments on these lands. This study identified densely stocked stands where thinning could provide a reliable source of wood, and examined the quantity, distribution, and economic value of the resulting timber for 5.5 million acres of national forest lands in eastern Oregon. Our findings verified local land managers' observations that the land base to support timber harvest targets in the region is smaller than anticipated in the past. Legal restrictions and current management practices have reduced the acreage available for harvest and mechanical restoration. Additionally, we found that on lands where active forestry is allowable, thinning of most densely stocked stands would not be economically viable. Findings from this analysis can help establish a common understanding of Blue Mountains vegetative and economic conditions for managers trying to restore the region's national forests.

Keywords: Blue Mountains, fuel reduction, timber, financial analysis, thinning.

Contents

Chapter 1: Introduction

Robert Rainville

The Purpose of This Assessment

Over the past 15 years, management of national forests in the Blue Mountains of eastern Oregon has changed immensely. Dramatically altered by decades of fire suppression and timber harvest, these forests no longer function as they once did. In response to insect and disease outbreaks, wildfires, and federal listings of wildlife and fish species, management emphasis has shifted from production of commercially valued timber to recovery of forested environments.

Dramatically altered by decades of fire suppression and timber harvest, these forests no longer function as they once did.

This change in direction has had a pronounced effect on the economic health of small communities located within the region. As managers began emphasizing recovery of forest conditions more like those found before Euro-American settlement, harvest of larger trees dropped dramatically. Rather than harvesting large trees, managers began removing small trees that were now abundant and that increased risks posed by wildfires and insects (Ager et al. 2007, Hemstrom et al. 2007, Hessburg et al. 1994). Since the early 1990s, the volume of timber removed from national forests in this region has declined dramatically. Although harvest levels on private (nonindustrial private forest and forest industry) land has stayed fairly constant (Adams and Latta 2003) (fig. 1-1), they do not come close to the volume removed from federal lands through the 1970s and 1980s. In response to a decreasing supply of larger timber, several timber mills closed and many logging companies disappeared. Hundreds of high-paying timber jobs were lost. In most communities, unemployment climbed to over 10 percent during the 1990s. As people left the area, social systems such as schools and hospitals were forced to reduce their services.

To arrest this trend, local leaders have sought to adjust their economies to better incorporate the change in forest products. Some forest products firms have shown a willingness to retool to use the smaller timber. Industries that utilize forest biomass (small unmerchantable trees and logging residue) have begun to assess opportunities. Any future investments from wood products industries will depend upon evaluations of the supply, composition, reliability, and value of timber that may become available from thinning treatments on national forest lands.

Private timber will play an important role in local economies in response to the dramatic decrease in harvest from federal lands. Solutions that are economically viable will most likely initially incorporate existing processing infrastructure, which is currently supplied largely from private land.

To assist communities, industries, and forest managers in planning for the future, former Oregon Governor Kitzhaber requested that Harv Forsgren, then

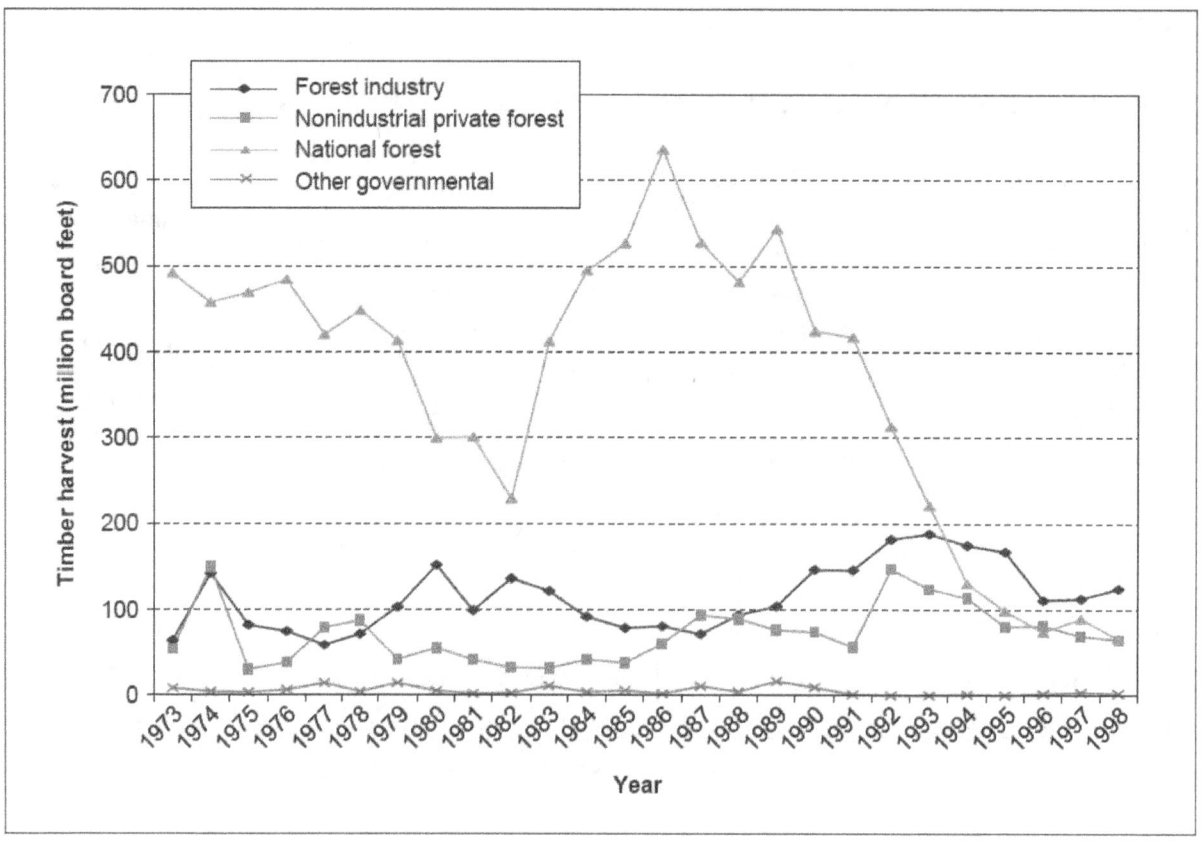

Figure 1-1—Harvest levels by ownership for the five counties in northeastern Oregon.

Regional Forester for the Pacific Northwest Region of the Forest Service, and Jim Brown, then State Forester for Oregon, cooperate in assessing the quality, quantity, and economic value of timber likely to result from forest management in the Blue Mountains of eastern Oregon. In a June 5, 2001, letter, the Governor requested that the agencies:

1. Describe "management actions over the last decade and provide a context for measuring our success,"

2. Prepare "maps that show current vegetation conditions where a reliable supply of wood could be available and show land areas that are suitable for this supply,"

3. Estimate "the quantity and type of forest timber products that would result from forest restoration actions…to encompass the four counties," and

4. Include "a market analysis for potential timber products and the associated economic impacts on individual communities."

To respond to these requests, a team of managers and scientists from the U.S. Department of Agriculture Forest Service Pacific Northwest Research Station, and Wallowa-Whitman, Malheur, and Umatilla National Forests, Oregon State University, and the Oregon Department of Forestry was assembled. They were asked to provide estimates for a study area that included 5.5 million acres of national forest lands located in Baker, Grant, Harney, Morrow, Umatilla, Union, and Wallowa Counties in eastern Oregon. Forest lands managed by the Malheur National Forest in Crook and Wheeler Counties were also included.

Many factors influence a region's economic condition, such as amenity migration, timber availability from private timberlands, changes in industry competitive status, and the ability adapt to changes. Based upon the Governor's direction, the team limited their study to the following four objectives, which define the scope of this report:

1. Identify densely stocked[1] stands where thinning activities could provide a reliable supply of wood for commercial uses.

2. Describe and quantify forest management activities on national forest lands since 1988 and evaluate the effect of these treatments on existing conditions.

3. Estimate the quantity, composition, and economic value of timber resulting from treating densely stocked stands within areas suitable for sustainable harvest.

4. Evaluate the effect of new and proposed policy changes on management's ability to thin densely stocked stands and reduce fire risk.

Work began in fall 2001. National forest results were presented to Governor Kitzhaber in November 2002.

A Summary of Historical Changes in Blue Mountain Forests Since Euro-American Settlement

The forests of the Blue Mountains have changed substantially since the time of the first Euro-American settlers. Historically, open, single-storied stands of ponderosa pine (*Pinus ponderosa* P. & C. Lawson) were abundant in the Blues (fig. 1-2). These stands likely occupied 20 to 50 percent of the overall landscape and accounted for 40 to 75 percent of the forests (Langston 1995, Quigley and Arbelbide 1997). Timber harvest and fire suppression have gradually transformed most of these open, park-like ponderosa pine stands.

---

[1] Densely stocked stands are defined here as stands with stocking of greater than 45 percent of the maximum stand density index or more than 300 trees per acre smaller than 4 inches at breast height.

USDA Forest Service, Pacific Northwest Region

Figure 1-2—A fire in a stand of old-growth ponderosa pine.

Commercial Logging

Commercial logging began in the 1870s when the transcontinental railroad linked the Blue Mountains to national lumber markets (fig. 1-3). Logging accelerated during the 1890s. Timber companies extended railroad lines into several drainages, and sawmills began to appear across the Blues (Wickman 1992). With the establishment of the national forests, harvest slowed on public lands. National forest timber was difficult to access and more costly to acquire. From 1905 until 1916, most commercial timber harvest in the Blues came from private lands.

This situation changed in the 1920s. National forests began offering large timber sales that focused on removal of commercially valuable stands of old-growth ponderosa pine. Heavy logging occurred throughout the decade and was only abated by the drop in the national economy and the oversupply of lumber that occurred in the 1930s (Langston 1995).

Logging on the national forests increased again in the 1940s. Harvest levels remained relatively high throughout the next four decades (1950s through 1980s), as forest managers raced to salvage insect-killed timber and provide lumber for a growing national market.

Figure 1-3—Early logging operation near Sumpter, Oregon.

From its beginning, logging preferentially removed large, old-growth ponderosa pine trees (Langston 1995). Management of the national forests emphasized efficient and productive forests capable of meeting the Nation's demands into the future (fig. 1-4). The emerging discipline of forestry at the time held that "inferior" diseased and decadent trees needed to be removed and replaced with young,

Figure 1-4—Early logging operation near Sumpter, Oregon.

As harvest of large old-growth ponderosa pine continued, the size of available pine gradually decreased on national forests.

healthy, rapidly growing trees. Generally, this meant replacing slower growing, old-growth ponderosa pine with young, faster growing stands (Langston 1995). Langston (1995) reported that logging of pine was so intense during the logging boom that started in the 1920s that it exceeded sustainable rates. On the Malheur National Forest, two large timber sales made 2 billion board feet of pine available out of an estimated supply of 7 billion board feet on the forest.

As harvest of large old-growth ponderosa pine continued, the size of available pine gradually decreased on national forests. The average ponderosa pine harvested on the Wallowa-Whitman National Forest in 1912 was 33 inches in diameter at breast height (d.b.h.). In 1992, the average size harvested was 19 inches d.b.h. The quantity of ponderosa pine harvested also decreased over time. On the Wallowa-Whitman National Forest, 57 percent of the timber by volume was ponderosa pine in 1906. In 1991, its volume was less than 20 percent. On the Umatilla National Forest, ponderosa pine was 34 percent of the harvest volume in 1931 and 16 percent in 1981 (Langston 1995).

Fire Suppression

Historically, frequent low-severity fires and dry conditions encouraged the development and maintenance of open, single-storied ponderosa pine stands. Low-severity fires, with return intervals of less than 25 years prevented less fire-tolerant Douglas-fir (*Pseudotsuga menziesii* (Mirb.) Franco), grand fir (*Abies grandis* Dougl. ex D. Don), and small pines from becoming established under more fire-tolerant stands of old-growth ponderosa pine and larch (*Larix* spp.).

Figure 1-5—Suppression of a low-intensity fire burning in a ponderosa pine stand on the Wallowa National Forest, about 1910.

Fire suppression that occurred throughout the 20th century changed the structure of these stands (Hessburg et al. 2005) (fig. 1-5). Shade-tolerant grand fir and Douglas-fir trees were able to grow and replace ponderosa pine on mixed-conifer sites. The gradual filling of canopy gaps in these stands encouraged shade-tolerant species to replace the shade-intolerant ponderosa pine. On pine sites, young pine trees became established under what had once been open, single-storied stands. The resulting increase in ladder fuels enhanced the likelihood of tree torching and crown fires (Peterson et al. 2005). In both mixed-conifer and pine sites, shrubs increased in abundance, and a deep layer of branches,

USDA Forest Service, Pacific Northwest Region

needles, and other decomposing organic material accumulated on the forest floor. This thick duff layer represents an important surface fuel (Johnson et al. 2007), capable of altering fire behavior and increasing soil heating. High soil temperatures can cause the mortality of large, old trees even if the tree crowns are not killed by a wildfire (Swezy and Agee 1991).

The extent of these changes has been dramatic. On the Wallowa-Whitman National Forest, about 71 percent of the stands were open, old-growth pine stands in 1912 (Langston 1995). A more recent vegetation survey estimates that 22 percent of these stands remained in 2005 (Countryman 2005). On the Umatilla National Forest, approximately 43 percent of the forest was open pine stands in 1905. In 2005, only 26 percent remained (Countryman 2005). Similarly, on the Malheur National Forest, open ponderosa pine stands accounted for 78 percent of the forests in 1938. In 2005, 18 percent of these stands remained (Countryman 2005).

Insect Outbreaks

As open, single-storied stands were converted to multistoried stands, and drought-tolerant ponderosa pine was replaced by grand fir and Douglas-fir, the frequency and intensity of insect outbreaks increased. In the Blue Mountains, annual precipitation averages 22 inches and ranges from 12 to 47 inches (Quigley and Arbelbide 1997). Drought is a common occurrence. Under the Blue Mountain's normal moisture-limited conditions, densely stocked stands of grand fir and Douglas-fir trees become stressed, increasing their vulnerability to insect infestation. Similarly, on pine sites, multistoried, densely stocked ponderosa pine stands are at risk to insect infestation under drought conditions. As these densely stocked and moisture-stressed stands became more abundant during the last half of the 20th century, localized insect infestations quickly blossomed into outbreaks covering thousands of acres (Fletcher et al. 1996, Gast et al. 1991).

A chronology of the types and extent of insect outbreaks that have occurred in the Blue Mountains since 1945 is displayed in table 1-1. Of the insects involved, the western spruce budworm (*Choristoneura occidentalis* Freeman), Douglas-fir tussock moth (*Orgyia pseudotsugata* McDunnough), Douglas-fir beetle (*Dendroctonus pseudotsugae* Hopkins), and fir engraver (*Scolytus ventralis* LeConte) attack Douglas-fir and grand fir trees. Although insect outbreaks likely occurred prior to the time of the first Euro-American settlers, the frequency and size of outbreaks caused by western spruce budworm species, and possibly other insects that attack Douglas-fir and grand fir, appear to have increased as a result of the proliferation of fir-dominated forests (Swetnam et al. 1995). Similarly, the multistoried ponderosa stands that replaced the single-storied stands on pine

As open, single-storied stands were converted to multistoried stands, and drought-tolerant ponderosa pine was replaced by grand fir and Douglas-fir, the frequency and intensity of insect outbreaks increased.

Table 1-1—Insect outbreaks in the Blue Mountains from 1945 to 1995

Year	Western spruce budworm (all forest ownerships)	Douglas-fir tussock moth (all forest ownerships)	Douglas-fir beetle (USFS lands only)	Mountain pine beetle (USFS lands only)	Spruce beetle (USFS lands only)	Fir engraver (USFS lands only)	Western pine beetle (USFS lands only)
1945	Maximum area 2.5 million acres			Maximum area 10,500 acres			
1946		Maximum area 120,000 acres					
1947							
1948							
1949							
1950			Maximum area 600,000 acres				
1951							
1952							
1953							Affected area ranged from 10,000 to 90,000 acres annually
1954							
1955							
1956					Maximum area 20,000 acres		
1957							
1958							
1959			Maximum area 75,000 acres				
1960							
1961							
1962		Maximum area 35,000 acres		Maximum area 50,000 acres			
1963							
1964			Maximum area 75,000 acres				
1965							
1966							
1967							
1968							
1969						Maximum area 240,000 acres	
1970							
1971							
1972		Maximum area 630,000 acres					
1973							
1974							
1975							
1976			Maximum area 145,000 acres	Maximum area 900,000 acres			
1977							
1978							
1979							
1980	Maximum area 3.8 million acres						
1981							
1982							
1983							
1984							
1985							
1986							
1987					Maximum area 70,000 acres		
1988			Maximum area 220,000 acres			Maximum area 275,000 acres	
1989							
1990							
1991		Maximum area 180,000 acres					Maximum area 78,000 acres
1992							
1993							
1994							
1995							

Sources: Gast et al. 1991 and Fletcher et al. 1996. Years and acres were interpolated from graphs prepared with Aerial Insect Detection Survey data from these publications.

sites have also increased the potential for outbreaks of the western pine beetle (*Dendroctonus brevicomis* LeContc) and mountain pine beetle (*D. ponderosae* Hopkins) (Hessburg et al. 1994).

Over the past 50 years, tree mortality from insect outbreaks has been high—often exceeding 80 percent (Swetnam et al. 1995). Although each outbreak was followed by an effort to salvage dead trees, low merchantability and limited access prevented removal of dead trees from many areas. The abundance of insect-killed trees substantially increased the surface fuel loads over thousands of acres across the Blue Mountains. Conditions became conducive for the occurrence of large, high-intensity wildfires. From 1985 until 1994, lightning-caused wildfires burned over 445,000 acres in the Blue Mountains (Fletcher et al. 1996). Many of these fires were hot, stand-replacement events that killed most of the trees over large areas.

As a consequence of this history, today's Blue Mountain forests are markedly different from those that existed a century earlier (Langston 1995). Open, single-storied ponderosa pine stands have decreased, while dense, multistoried stands of Douglas-fir and true fir have increased. Today, more stands are dominated by young to mid-aged trees as a result of selective harvesting of larger trees, salvage logging, and regeneration harvests that followed insect and wildfire mortality. Risk of insect outbreaks is higher now because of an abundance of densely stocked mixed-species stands. The probability of large, high-intensity, stand-replacing wildfires is greater as a result of the increase in insect-induced tree mortality, the large acreage of multistoried stands composed of fire-intolerant true fir species, and the accumulation of duff and shrubs on the forest floor.

The abundance of insect-killed trees substantially increased the surface fuel loads over thousands of acres across the Blue Mountains. Conditions became conducive for the occurrence of large, high-intensity wildfires.

Metric Equivalents

When you know:	Multiply by:	To find:
Inches	2.54	Centimeters
Acres	.405	Hectares
Billion board feet	5.67	Million cubic meters

Literature Cited

Adams, D.M.; Latta, G. 2003. Private timber harvest in eastern Oregon. Res. Contrib. 42. Corvallis, OR: Oregon State University, College of Forestry, Forest Research Laboratory. 42 p.

Ager, A.A.; MacMahan, A.; Hayes, J.L.; Smith, E. 2007. Modeling the effects of thinning on bark beetle impacts and wildfire potential in the Blue Mountains of eastern Oregon. Landscape and Urban Planning. 80: 301–311.

Countryman, B. 2005. Personal communication. Vegetation specialist, Blue Mountains Forest Plan Revision Team, 1550 Dewey Avenue, P.O. Box 907, Baker City, OR 97814.

Fletcher, S.L.; Howes, S.W.; Scott, D.W.; Schmitt, C.L.; Szymoniak, J.; Gast, W.R.; Crompton, D.; Brooks, P. 1996. Forest health update: five years later. Monitoring report to the Forest Supervisor, Wallowa-Whitman National Forest. On file with: Umatilla National Forest, Forest Planning, 2517 SW Hailey Ave., Pendleton, OR 97801.

Gast, W.R., Jr.; Scott, D.W.; Schmitt, C.; Clemens, D.; Howes, S.; Johnson, C.G., Jr.; Mason, R.; Mohr, F. 1991. Blue Mountains forest health report: new perspectives in forest health. Portland, OR: U.S. Department of Agriculture, Forest Service, Pacific Northwest Region, Malheur, Umatilla, and Wallowa-Whitman National Forests.

Hemstrom, M.A.; Merzenich, J.; Reger, A.; Wales, B. 2007. Integrated analysis of landscape management scenarios using state and transition models in the upper Grande Ronde River subbasin, Oregon, USA. Landscape and Urban Planning. 80: 198–211.

Hessburg, P.F.; Agee, J.K.; Franklin, J.F. 2005. Dry forests and wildland fires of the inland Northwest USA: contrasting the landscape ecology of the pre-settlement and modern eras. Forest Ecology and Management. 211: 117–139.

Hessburg, P.F.; Mitchell, R.G.; Filip, G.M. 1994. Historical and current roles of insects and pathogens in eastern Oregon and Washington forested landscapes. Gen. Tech. Rep. PNW-GTR-327. Portland, OR: U.S. Department of Agriculture, Forest Service, Pacific Northwest Research Station. 72 p.

Johnson, M.C.; Peterson, D.L.; Raymond, C.L. 2007. Guide to fuel treatments in dry forests of the Western United States: assessing forest structure and fire hazard. Gen. Tech. Rep. PNW-GTR-686. Portland, OR: U.S. Department of Agriculture, Forest Service, Pacific Northwest Research Station. 322 p.

Langston, N. 1995. Forest dreams, forest nightmares: the paradox of old growth in the inland West. Seattle, WA: University of Washington Press. 368 p.

Peterson, D.L.; Johnson, M.C.; Agee, J.K.; Jain, T.B.; McKenzie, D.; Reinhardt, E.D. 2005. Forest structure and fire hazard in dry forests of the Western United States. Gen. Tech. Rep. PNW-GTR-628. Portland, OR: U.S. Department of Agriculture, Forest Service, Pacific Northwest Research Station. 30 p.

Quigley, T.M.; Arbelbide, S.J., tech. eds. 1997. An assessment of ecosystem components in the interior Columbia basin and portions of the Klamath and Great Basins. Gen. Tech. Rep. PNW-GTR-405. Portland, OR: U.S. Department of Agriculture, Forest Service, Pacific Northwest Research Station. 718 p. Vol. 2.

Swetnam, T.W.; Wickman, B.H.; Paul, G.; Baisan, C.H. 1995. Historical patterns of western spruce budworm and Douglas-fir tussock moth outbreaks in the northern Blue Mountains, Oregon since A.D. 1700. Res. Pap. PNW-RP-484. Portland, OR: U.S. Department of Agriculture, Forest Service, Pacific Northwest Research Station. 27 p.

Swezy, D.M.; Agee, J.K. 1991. Prescribed-fire effects on fine-root and tree mortality in old-growth ponderosa pine. Canadian Journal of Forest Research. 21: 626–634.

Wickman, B.E. 1992. Forest health in the Blue Mountains: the influence of insects and diseases. Gen. Tech. Rep. PNW-GTR-295. Portland, OR: U.S. Department of Agriculture, Forest Service, Pacific Northwest Research Station. 15 p.

Chapter 2: Location of Densely Stocked Stands[1] Where Thinning Activities Could Provide a Reliable Supply of Wood for Commercial Uses

Michael Braymen, Jerome Hensley, Donald Justice, Anne Kramer, William McArthur, David Powell, Victoria Rockwell, and Edward Uebler

Introduction

All national forest land in the Blue Mountains is managed to achieve resource objectives established in forest land and resource management plans in accordance with agency policies and federal laws. Achievement of some resource objectives prohibit or significantly inhibit the use of silvicultural treatments such as thinning. For example, commercial thinning of dense stands in wilderness areas, sensitive species habitat, inventoried roadless areas, or Wild and Scenic River corridors is prohibited or would require considerable environmental analysis and documentation (USDA Forest Service 1990a, 1990b, 1990c).

To assess whether commercial thinning could be a viable tool in returning the landscape to conditions that are less susceptible to insect outbreaks and uncharacteristic stand-replacement fires, managers need to know the size and location of stands in need of treatment. With this information, they can determine whether these stands are located in management areas where commercial thinning is prohibited or restricted by land management plans, policies, or laws.

Thinning can be an effective tool to alter vegetative conditions in ways that will change fire behavior under the conditions found in the Blue Mountains (Ager et al. 2005). Thinning can also increase or decrease the likelihood of insect outbreaks, depending on how it is implemented (Ager et al. 2007). For managers to use thinning as a viable tool to alter conditions across a landscape, there must be some realizable economic value from the trees harvested. Managers need to know to what extent thinning dense stands will result in positive net revenues (Fight and Barbour 2006).

The location and geographic distribution of densely stocked stands influences the financial feasibility of employing thinning as a recovery tool on a landscape basis (fig. 2-1). If treatable areas are in small, scattered blocks, far from roads, or

For managers to use thinning as a viable tool to alter conditions across a landscape, there must be some realizable economic value from the trees harvested

---

[1] Densely stocked stands are defined here as stands with stocking of greater than 45 percent of the maximum stand density index or more than 300 trees per acre smaller than 4 inches at breast height.

USDA Forest Service, Pacific Northwest Region

Figure 2-1—Diverse Blue Mountain forest landscape.

would require long yarding and haul distances, it is less likely that thinning treatments will be feasible without subsidization. Under these conditions, the possibility that a sustainable timber industry could be a part of the process of creating a forest that is more resilient to fire and insects would be unlikely. Subsidies or technological changes would be needed before more widespread commercial use would be financially viable. New management tools such as stewardship contracting authority (the ability to trade timber for forestry work) may influence this situation.

Methods

Management allocations established in 1990 forest land and resource management plans (USDA Forest Service 1990a, 1990b, 1990c) were used to identify lands that are suitable for providing a reliable supply of wood for commercial uses. Forest plan allocations were assigned to one of five management area categories (MACs) based upon the relative likelihood that timber removed during thinning activities would contribute timber outputs for local industries. The appendix describes which forest plan management allocations were included in each MAC.

Management area categories include:

- **Nonforest** includes rock, water, grasslands, shrublands, juniper, roads, and lands with less than 10 percent tree canopy closure. Thinning treatments were assumed to be unnecessary in these areas.

- **Reserves** are lands where timber harvest is prohibited by law, regulation, or forest plan requirement. National forest plans include these acres in the unregulated timber base. No timber production was assumed for these areas.

- **Restricted** lands are areas where restrictions on timber harvest have been implemented through forest plan amendments or agency policy. Included are riparian, roadless, and old-growth (late- and old-forest structure) areas that lie within management allocations where forest plans would otherwise permit timber harvest. Timber outputs from the restricted MAC were assumed to be insignificant owing to management costs, pubic controversy, or the importance placed on resource objectives that conflict with the production of sustainable and significant quantities of timber.

- **Lynx habitat** includes portions of management allocations where scheduled timber harvest may occur but where requirements for lynx (*Lynx canadensis* Kerr) habitat take priority. Although these lands are part of the regulated timber base in national forest plans, insignificant and unreliable timber production was assumed for these areas based upon experience. In April 2005, the U.S. Department of Agriculture Forest Service and the U.S. Fish and Wildlife Service revised the Lynx Conservation Agreement so that it only applies to "occupied habitat"; however, prior to this revision, little timber harvest was occurring within potential as well as occupied lynx habitat. The mapped lynx habitat on the Umatilla, Malheur, and Wallowa-Whitman National Forests is unoccupied. Unless new information verifies lynx presence, the Conservation Agreement will not apply in these areas (USDA Forest Service and USDI Fish and Wildlife Service 2006).

- **Active forestry** includes lands where scheduled timber harvest may occur and substantial and sustainable supplies of timber products are anticipated. Mechanical treatments are generally compatible with resource direction for lands in this category. National forest plans describe these lands as the regulated timber base.

The MACs were identified and mapped sequentially in the following order: nonforest, reserved, restricted, lynx, active forestry. An area that qualifies for more than one MAC (e.g., areas that are roadless areas [restricted MAC] and also lynx habitat) will be included in the MAC that was mapped first. As a result, acreage displayed for MACs identified and mapped later in the sequential order may be less than the total number of acres that meet that MAC description.

Landscape-level assessments were used to identify the location of individual stands within the active forestry, restricted, and lynx habitat MACs. On the Umatilla and Wallowa-Whitman National Forests, lands were mapped through interpretation of aerial photos or stand information from the existing vegetation (EVG) database. The potential vegetation type or plant association of each stand was determined for forested areas. Similar potential vegetation types and plant associations were aggregated into biophysical groups or plant associations.

Stocking thresholds were determined for each biophysical group in the Blue Mountains province by using methods described in Cochran et al. (1994) and Powell (1999). If the site could support more than one tree species, the stocking threshold for the most limiting species was used to represent the biophysical group. Stocking information for each stand was compared to the appropriate stocking threshold to locate densely stocked conditions. If stand information on numbers of trees or basal area per acre were not available, canopy closure was used as a surrogate for stand density and stand density thresholds. No attempt was made to estimate high-density stand conditions for stands dominated by seedlings and saplings because this method does not work well in these small-diameter tree stands.

On the Malheur National Forest, Landsat satellite images and forest activity databases were used to locate densely stocked stands. To estimate existing conditions, 1990 Landsat data were adjusted to account for large wildfires, timber harvest, and timber stand improvement activities that had occurred since 1990. Densely stocked conditions were assumed to exist in stands with forested canopy closures greater than 40 percent. Old-growth forest conditions were identified by using a size/structure classification. Stands where more than 10 percent of the canopy is occupied by size classes with trees larger than 20 inches diameter at breast height were considered old growth.

Results

National forest acreages associated with each MAC are shown in table 2-1 and the totals for the three national forests are displayed in figure 2-2.

Table 2-1—Acreage of Blue Mountain national forests in each management area category

Management area category	Malheur National Forest		Umatilla National Forest		Wallowa-Whitman National Forest		Total	
	Acres	*Percent*	*Acres*	*Percent*	*Acres*	*Percent*	*Acres*	*Percent*
Nonforest	484,000	29	188,000	13	727,000	30	1,400,000	26
Reserved	248,000	15	483,000	34	648,000	27	1,378,000	25
Restricted	312,000	18	180,000	13	426,000	18	918,000	17
Lynx	7,000	<1	105,000	8	76,000	3	189,000	3
Active forestry	647,000	38	452,000	32	517,000	22	1,616,000	29
Total	1,698,000		1,408,000		2,394,000		5,500,000	

Source: National forest geographic information maps.

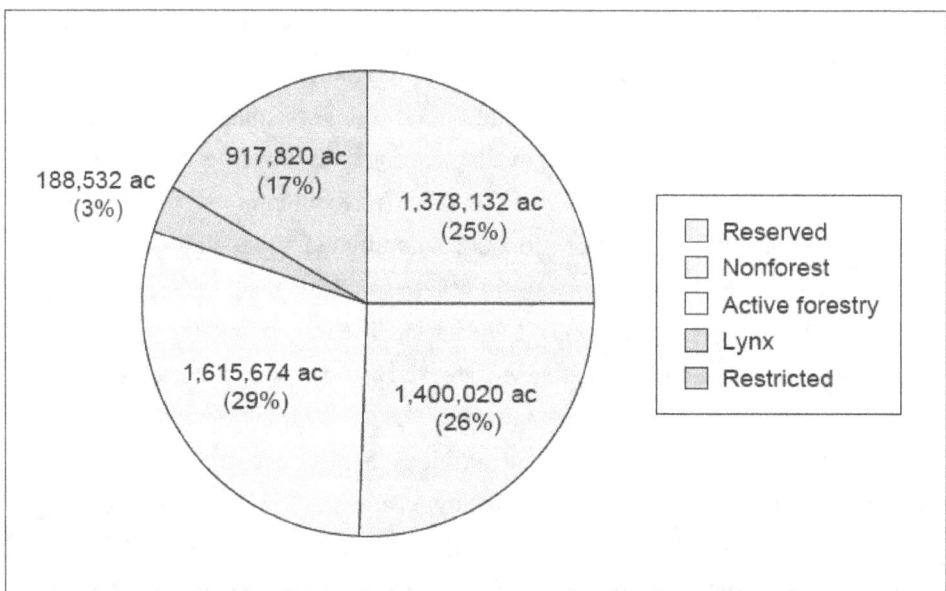

Figure 2-2—Availability of national forest lands in Blue Mountain forests for significant and sustainable timber production.

Figures 2-3, 2-4, and 2-5 show the large acreage of reserve, nonforest, and restricted MACs on each forest. The active forestry MACs on each national forest are widely distributed outside reserve MACs and are often interspersed with restricted MAC riparian and old-growth areas.

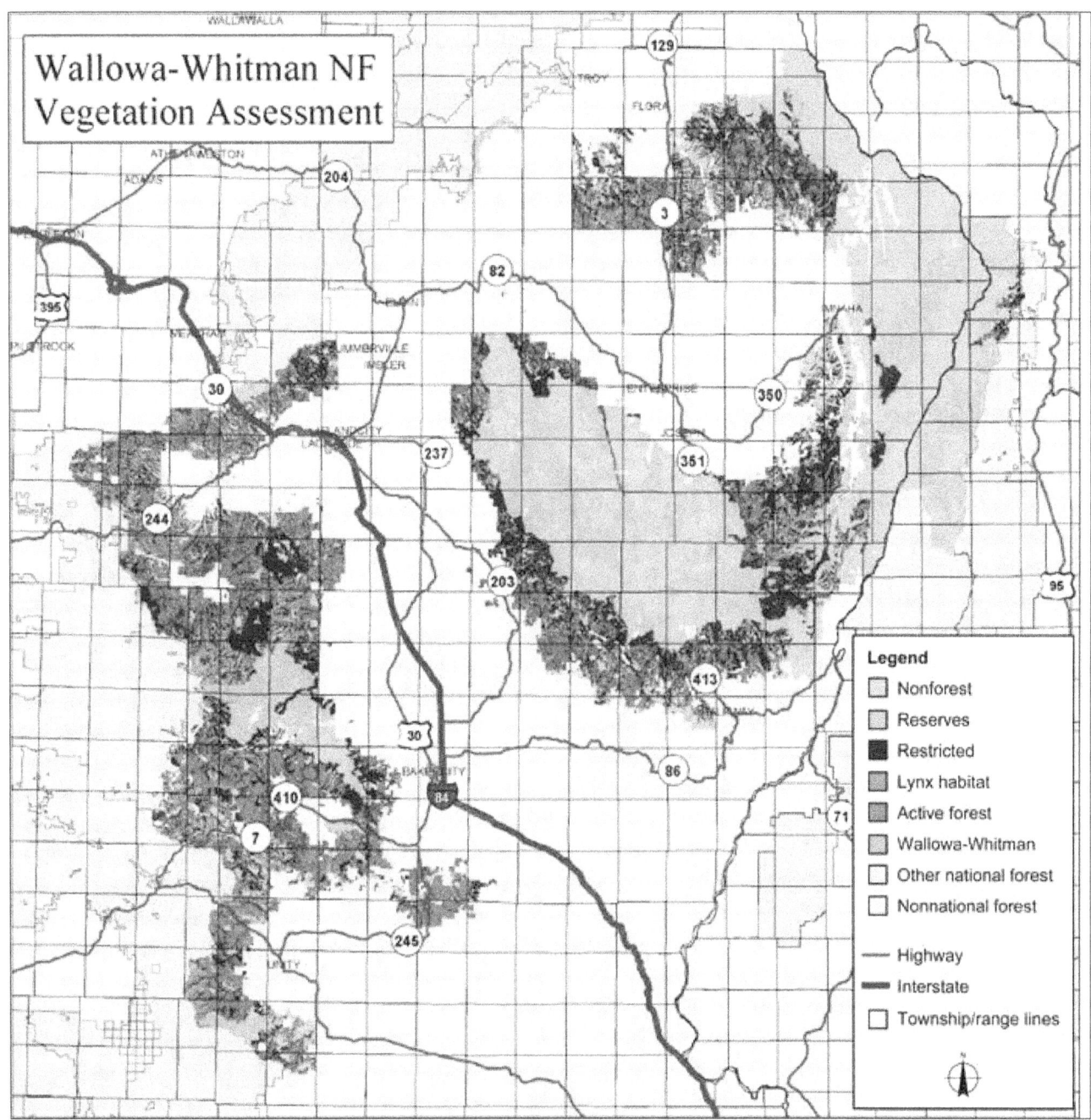

Figure 2-3—Timber availability categories for the Wallowa-Whitman National Forest.

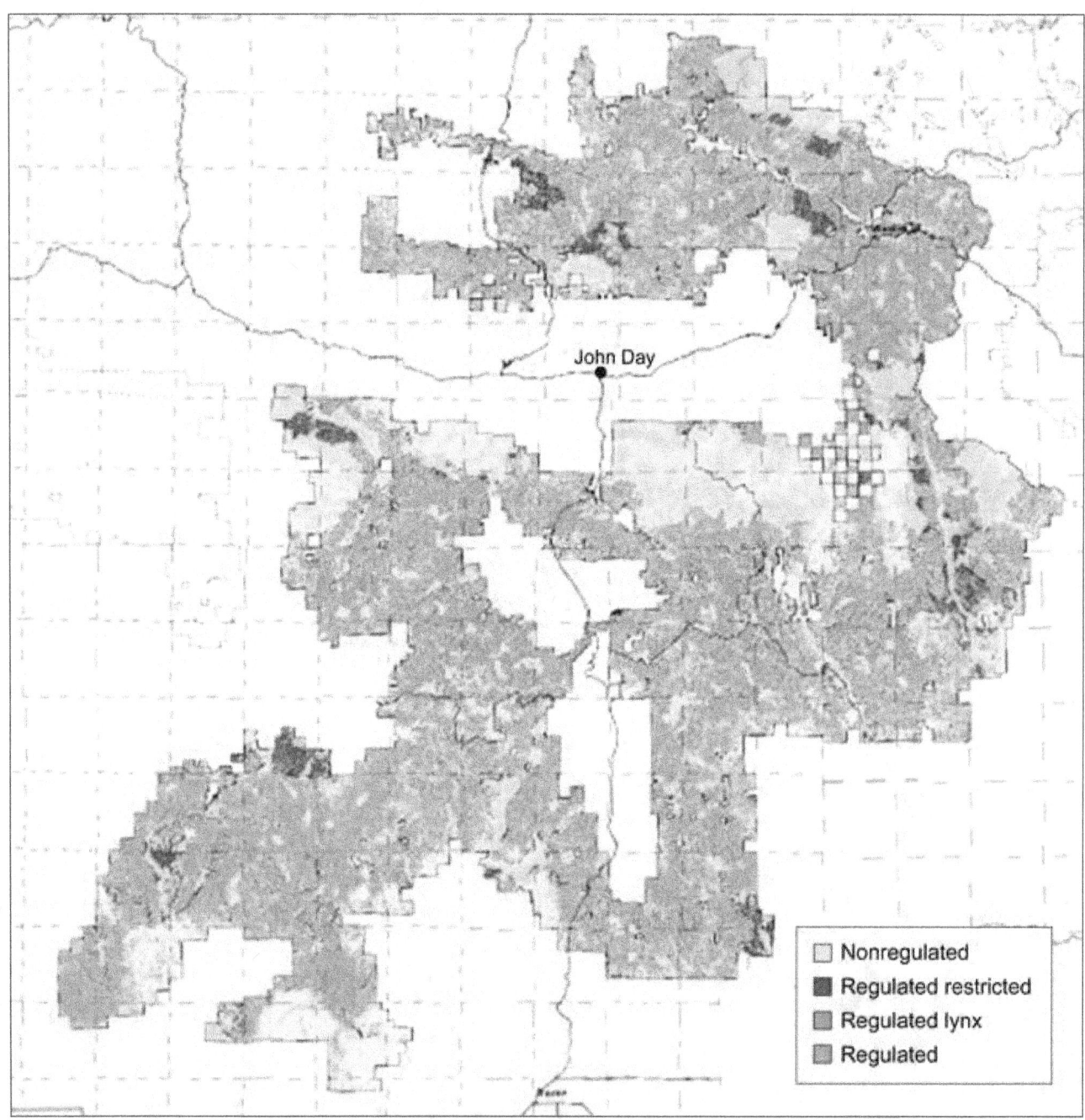

Figure 2-4—Timber availability categories for the Malheur National Forest.

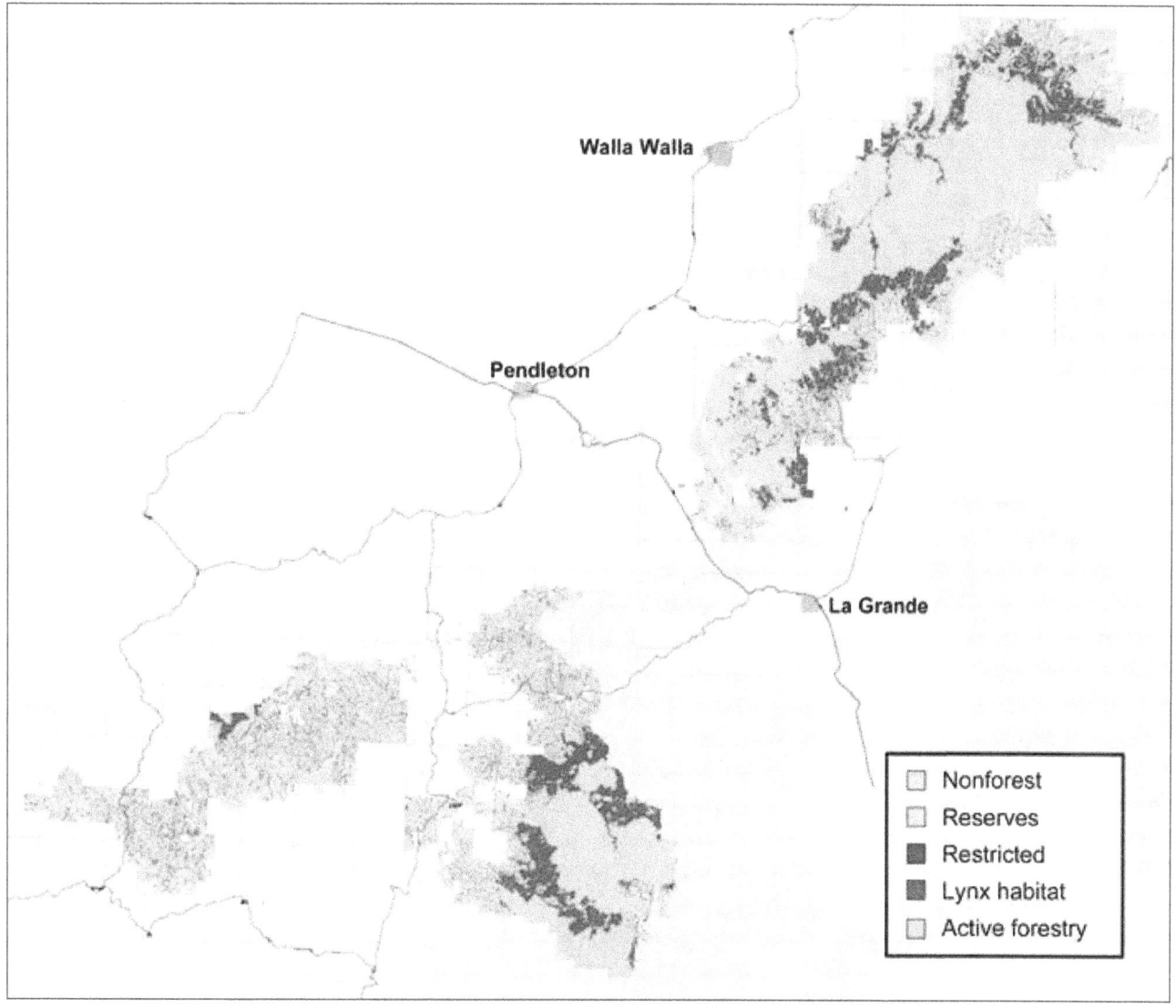

Figure 2-5—Timber availability categories for the Umatilla National Forest.

A fragmented distribution emerges when the densely stocked stands within the active forest and restricted MACs are located on the national forests (figs. 2-6, 2-7, and 2-8). Some concentrated blocks were identified north and west of the town of Unity, northwest of the town of Burns, north and northeast of Prairie City, and near the towns of Seneca and Ukiah; however, across most of the national forest lands, densely stocked stands are widely distributed.

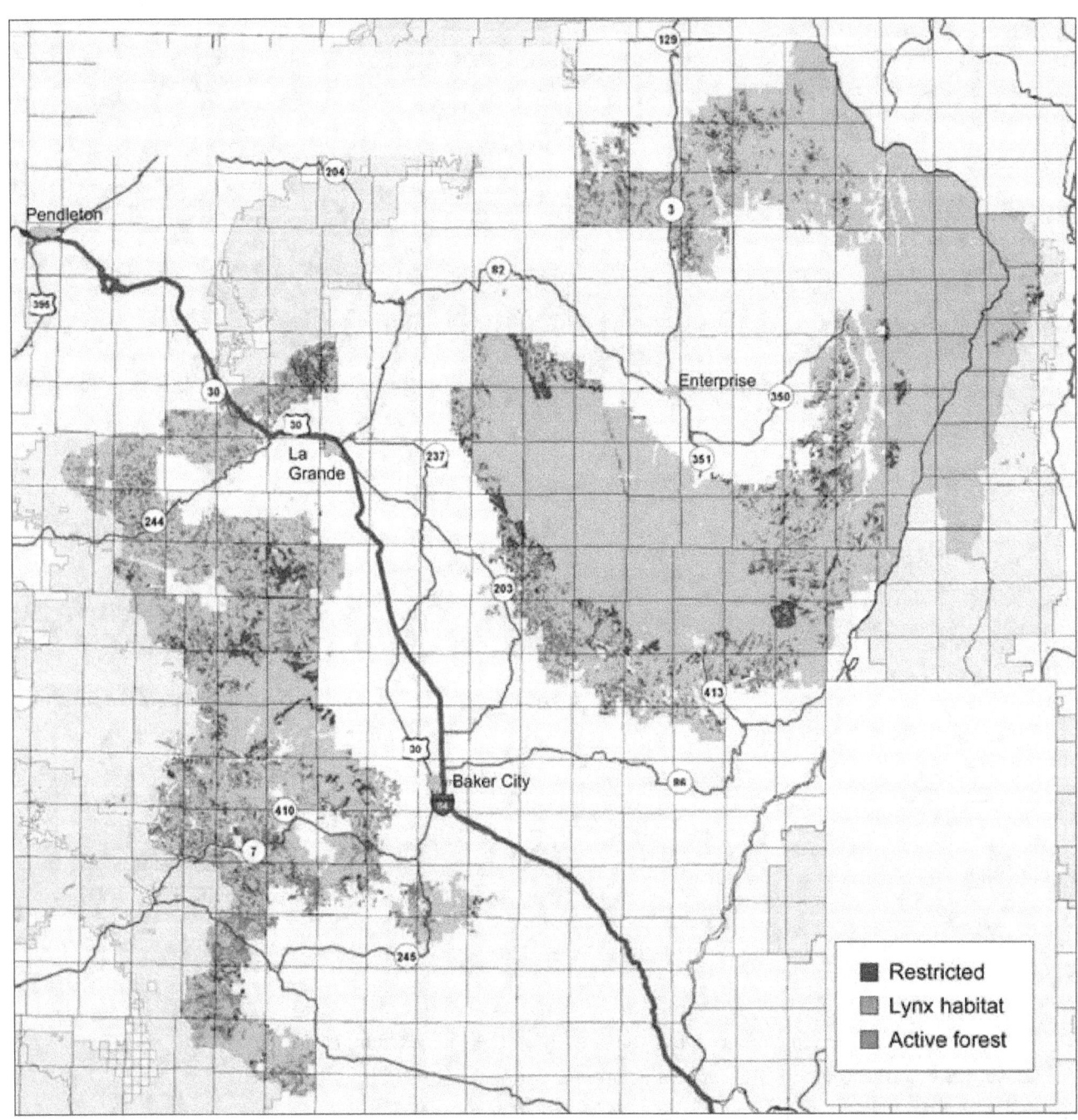

Figure 2-6—Densely stocked stands on the Wallowa-Whitman National Forest.

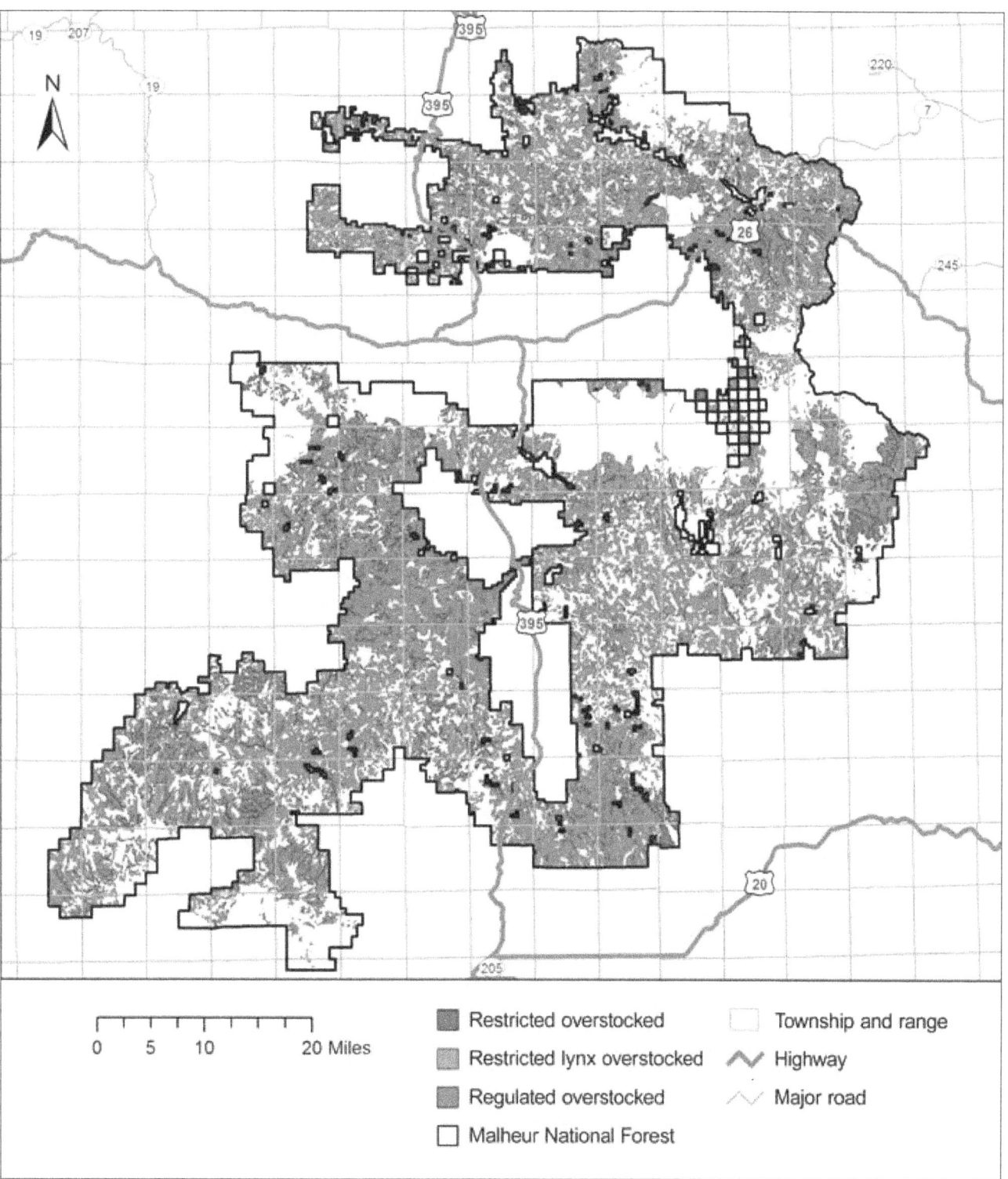

Figure 2-7—Densely stocked stands on the Malheur National Forest. Map by Theresa Burcsu. Note: this map is not the original, but was re-created to improve its visual quality.

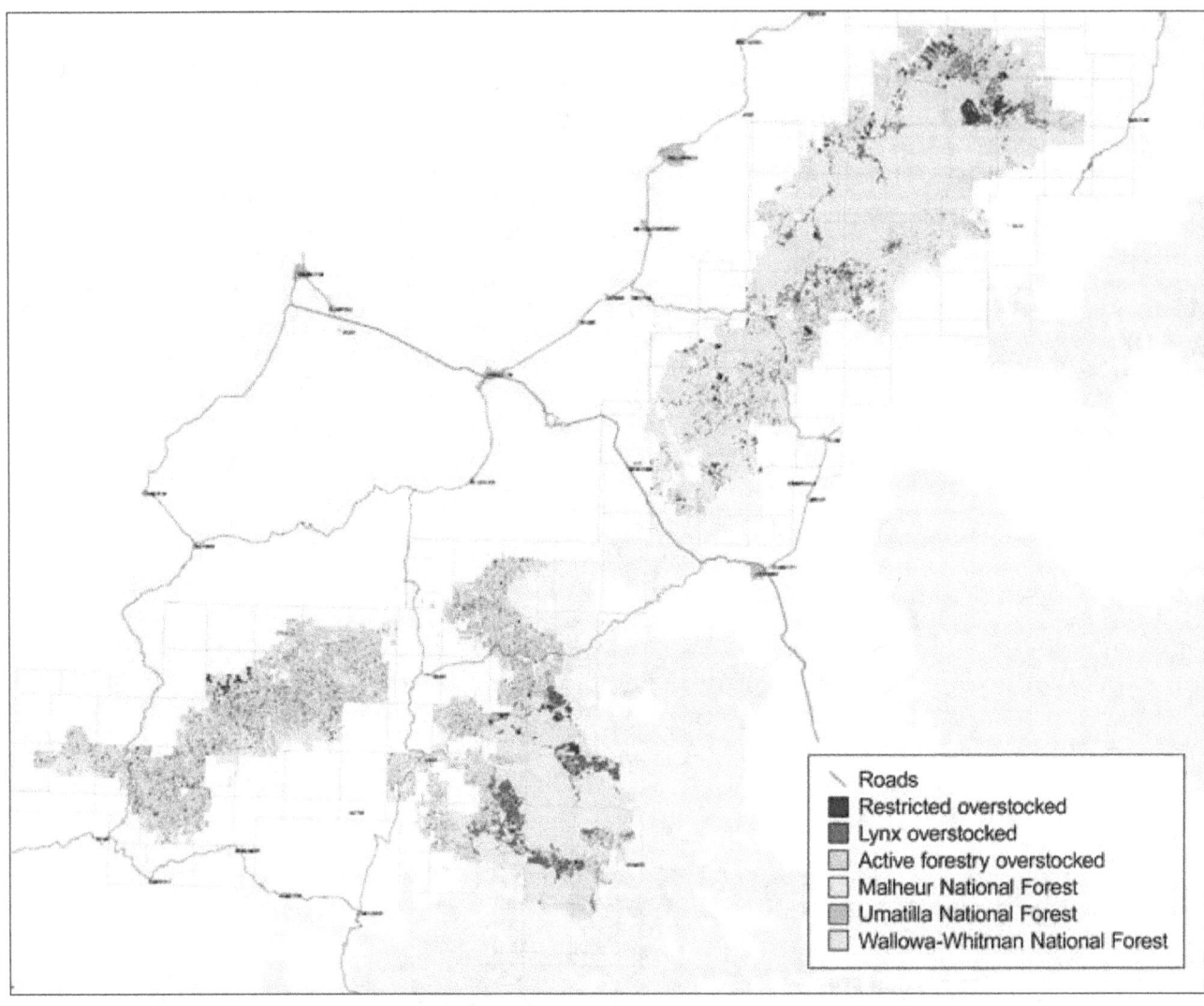

Figure 2-8—Densely stocked stands on the Umatilla National Forest.

Discussion

About one-fourth of the 5.5 million acres of land administered by the U.S. Department of Agriculture Forest Service in the Blue Mountains is not forested (fig. 2-2). In the 46 percent of the three Blue Mountains national forests that is forested, thinning with timber removal is an unlikely treatment method. This does not mean that other vegetative management options (prescribed fire, wildland fire use, or thinning without commercial timber removal) could not be used to reduce fire hazard, but it is doubtful that these areas would produce much commercial timber. On the other hand, about 29 percent (1.6 million acres) is still available for active forestry.

When the MACs are evaluated on a forest-by-forest basis, the results differ only slightly (table 2-1). The area available for timber management ranges from a high of 38 percent (647,000 acres) on the Malheur National Forest to a low of 22 percent (517,000 acres) on the Wallowa-Whitman National Forest. There are, however, important differences among the three forests. A considerably smaller proportion of the Umatilla National Forest is nonforest (13 percent) compared to other national forests, and the Malheur National Forest has only about half as much of its total area (15 percent) in the reserved MAC as the other forests.

Only densely stocked stands within the active forestry MAC were considered suitable for contributing a reliable supply of wood for commercial uses. Harvest from other MACs such as restricted or lynx may occur, but outputs from these lands will likely be low and unpredictable owing to other resource objectives and public controversy (USDA Forest Service and USDI Fish and Wildlife Service 2006).

In most cases, stands in need of treatment are widely scattered.

The distribution of the densely stocked stands within the active forest MAC will present challenges to management. In most cases, stands in need of treatment are widely scattered. A few larger blocks exist, but they are the exception. The fragmented nature of the densely stocked stands will result in increased transportation costs. More roads will be needed to access stands. The volume of harvested material will be transported on more miles of road than if the densely stocked stands were located in blocks. This situation will increase operation costs and prohibit treatment of some stands through traditional federal contracting methods.

Conclusions

Vegetative thinning on 1,616,000 acres (29 percent) of the Blue Mountain national forests could contribute substantial and sustainable timber products for local communities. Timber harvest would need to be compatible with site-specific resource needs and be feasible economically. This report represents a snapshot in time and does not address long-term changes that will occur nor the duration of harvest, i.e., whether these acres would be cut over a decade or over a century.

Timber harvest would need to be compatible with site-specific resource needs and be feasible economically.

Restricted and lynx MACs account for 1,107,000 acres (20 percent). Although some timber products could result from treatments within these areas, outputs will likely be low and unpredictable because of the controversial nature of timber harvest and thinning treatments within lynx, riparian, and old-growth areas. Faced with limited budgets, national forest managers will likely focus their restoration efforts in less controversial areas.

No commercial timber outputs are anticipated from the 2,778,000 acres (51 percent of the total area) of reserved and nonforest lands. Changes in forest plan or congressional designations would be needed for commercial timber harvest to become a possibility.

Management of densely stocked stands in the active forest MAC will be challenging owing to the distribution of these lands. The scattered nature of these lands will increase transportation costs and prevent treatment of some stands because of high costs, low revenues, or a combination of the two.

Metric Equivalents

When you know:	Multiply by:	To find:
Inches	2.54	Centimeters
Feet	.305	Meters
Acres	.405	Hectares

Literature Cited

Ager, A.A.; Barbour, R.J.; Hayes, J.L. 2005. Examination of long-term fuels management scenarios on a wildland-urban interface in northeastern Oregon. In: Bevers, M.; Barrett, T.M, comps. Systems analysis in forest resources: proceedings of the 2003 symposium. Gen. Tech. Rep. PNW-GTR-656. Portland, OR: U.S. Department of Agriculture, Forest Service, Pacific Northwest Research Station: 215–228.

Ager, A.A.; McMahan, A.; Hayes, J.L.; Smith, E.L. 2007. Modeling the effects of thinning on bark beetle impacts and wildfire potential in the Blue Mountains of eastern Oregon. Landscape and Urban Planning. 80: 301–311.

Cochran, P.H.; Geist, J.M.; Clemens, D.L.; Clausnitzer, R.; Powell, D.C. 1994. Suggested stocking levels for forest stands in northeastern Oregon and southeastern Washington. Res. Note RN-513. Portland, OR: U.S. Department of Agriculture, Forest Service, Pacific Northwest Research Station. 21 p.

Fight, R.D.; Barbour, R.J. 2006. Financial analysis of fuel treatments on national forests in the Western United States. Res. Note. PNW-RN-555. Portland, OR: U.S. Department of Agriculture, Forest Service, Pacific Northwest Research Station. 10 p.

Powell, D.C. 1999. Suggested stocking levels for forest stands in northeastern Oregon and southeastern Washington: an implementation guide for the Umatilla National Forest. F14-SO-TP-03-1999. Pendleton, OR: U.S. Department of Agriculture, Forest Service, Pacific Northwest Region, Umatilla National Forest. 72 p.

U.S. Department of Agriculture, Forest Service. 1990a. Malheur National Forest land and resource management plan and record of decision. John Day, OR: Malheur National Forest, Pacific Northwest Region. 171 p.

U.S. Department of Agriculture, Forest Service. 1990b. Umatilla National Forest land and resource management plan and record of decision. Pendleton, OR: Umatilla National Forest, Pacific Northwest Region. 373 p.

U.S. Department of Agriculture, Forest Service. 1990c. Wallowa-Whitman National Forest land and resource management plan and record of decision. Baker, OR: Wallowa-Whitman National Forest, Pacific Northwest Region. 415 p.

U.S. Department of Agriculture, Forest Service; U.S. Department of the Interior, Fish and Wildlife Service. 2006. Letter to forest supervisors: Okanogan-Wenatchee, Colville, Umatilla, Malheur, and Wallowa-Whitman National Forests. Revised lynx conservation agreement. File code 2670/1950. On file with: Pacific Northwest Research Station, 333 SW First Avenue, Portland, OR 97204.

Appendix: Assignment of 1990 Forest Land and Resources Management Plan Allocations to Management Area Categories

Nonforest Management Area Category

Rock, water, grasslands, shrublands, juniper, roads (including a 33-foot-wide zone) and forested stands with less than 10 percent tree cover were considered nonforested.

Reserved Management Area Category

Allocation number	Allocation name
Malheur National Forest:	
3A	Non-anadromous riparian
3B	Anadromous riparian
5	Bald eagle (*Haliaeetus leucocephalus* Linn.) winter roosts
6A	Strawberry Mountain Wilderness
6B	Monument Rock Wilderness
7	Scenic
8	Special interest
9	Research natural area
10	Semiprimitive nonmotorized recreation
11	Semiprimitive motorized recreation
13	Old growth
17	Byram Gulch municipal supply watershed
18	Long Creek municipal supply watershed
21	Wildlife emphasis area with nonscheduled timber harvest
22	Wild and scenic river
Ochoco National Forest administered by the Malheur National Forest:	
1	Wilderness
2	Wilderness
3	Wilderness
4	Wilderness
5	Research natural areas
6	Old growth
7	Trail
10	Silver Creek
12	Eagle roost
13	Developed recreation
15	Riparian
28	Facilities

Umatilla National Forest:

A1	Nonmotorized dispersed recreation
A2	Off-highway vehicle recreation
A6	Developed recreation
A7	Wild and scenic rivers (wild portion only)
A8	Scenic area
A9	Special interest area
B1	Wilderness
C1	Dedicated old growth
C3A	Sensitive big game winter range
C7	Special fish management area (inside riparian only)
C8	Grass-tree mosaic
D2	Research natural area
F2	Mill Creek municipal watershed
F4	Walla Walla River watershed (unroaded portion only)

Wallowa-Whitman National Forest:

4	Wilderness
6	Roadless recreation (backcountry)
7	Wild and scenic rivers (wild portions only)
8	Hell's Canyon National Recreation Area (HCNRA) Snake River Corridor
9	HCNRA dispersed recreation/native vegetation
10	HCNRA forage
12	Research natural areas
13	Homestead Further Planning Area
14	Starkey Experimental Forest and Range
15	Old-growth forest
16	Administrative and recreation sites

Restricted Management Area Category

These restricted areas resulted from amendments to the Forest Land and Resources Management plans after the original records of decisions were signed in 1990. They include riparian habitat conservation areas (RHCA buffers), Regional Forester's amendment #2 (late and old structure), and roadless areas. Restricted areas are located within the following management allocations.

Allocation number	Allocation name
Malheur National Forest:	
1	General forest
2	Rangeland
4A	Big game winter range
12	Developed recreation sites
14	Visual corridors
19	Administrative sites
20A	Dry Cabin wildlife emphasis
20B	Utley Butte wildlife emphasis

27

Ochoco National Forest administered by the Malheur National Forest:

14	Dispersed recreation
20	Winter range
21	General forest winter range
22	General forest
26	Visuals

Umatilla National Forest:

A3	Viewshed 1
A4	Viewshed 2
A5	Roaded natural
A7	Wild and scenic rivers (scenic portion only)
A10	Wenaha-Tucannon special management area
C2	Managed old growth
C3	Big game winter range
C4	Wildlife habitat
C5	Riparian
C7	Special fish management area (outside riparian)
E1	Timber and forage
E2	Timber and big game
F3	High Ridge evaluation area
F4	Walla Walla River watershed (roaded portion only)

Wallowa-Whitman National Forest:

1 and 1w	Timber emphasis
3 and 3a	Big game habitat emphasis
5	Phillip's Lake area
7	Wild and scenic rivers (scenic portions only)
11	HCNRA dispersed recreation/timber management
17	Utility corridors
18	Anadromous fish emphasis

Lynx Management Area Category

In lynx habitat, scheduled timber harvest is restricted to provide denning and forage habitat for lynx. Lynx habitat that is located outside the restricted or reserved management area categories is within the following management allocations.

Allocation number	Allocation name
Malheur National Forest:	
1	General forest
2	Rangeland
4A	Big game winter range
12	Developed recreation sites
14	Visual corridors
19	Administrative sites
20A	Dry Cabin wildlife emphasis
20B	Utley Butte wildlife emphasis

Ochoco National Forest administered by the Malheur National Forest:

14	Dispersed recreation
20	Winter range
21	General forest winter range
22	General forest
26	Visuals

Umatilla National Forest:

A3	Viewshed 1
A4	Viewshed 2
A5	Roaded natural
A7	Wild and scenic rivers (scenic portion only)
A10	Wenaha-Tucannon special management area
C2	Managed old growth
C3	Big game winter range
C4	Wildlife habitat
C5	Riparian
C7	Special fish management area (outside riparian)
E1	Timber and forage
E2	Timber and big game
F3	High Ridge evaluation area
F4	Walla Walla River watershed (roaded portion only)

Wallowa-Whitman National Forest:

1 and 1w	Timber emphasis
3 and 3a	Big game habitat emphasis
5	Phillip's Lake area
7	Wild and scenic rivers (scenic portions only)
11	HCNRA dispersed recreation/timber management
17	Utility corridors
18	Anadromous fish emphasis

Active Forestry Management Area Category

Lands where scheduled timber harvest is permitted without the additional restrictions resulting from lynx habitat management or amendments to the forest plans are located in the following management allocations.

Allocation number	Allocation name
Malheur National Forest:	
1	General forest
2	Rangeland
4A	Big game winter range
12	Developed recreation sites
14	Visual corridors
19	Administrative sites
20A	Dry Cabin wildlife emphasis
20B	Utley Butte wildlife emphasis

Ochoco National Forest administered by the Malheur National Forest:

14	Dispersed recreation
20	Winter range
21	General forest winter range
22	General forest
26	Visuals

Umatilla National Forest:

A3	Viewshed 1
A4	Viewshed 2
A5	Roaded natural
A7	Wild and scenic rivers (scenic portion only)
A10	Wenaha-Tucannon special management area
C2	Managed old growth
C3	Big game winter range
C4	Wildlife habitat
C5	Riparian
C7	Special fish management area (outside riparian)
E1	Timber and forage
E2	Timber and big game
F3	High Ridge evaluation area
F4	Walla Walla River watershed (roaded portion only)

Wallowa-Whitman National Forest:

1 and 1w	Timber emphasis
3	MA3a—Big game habitat emphasis
5	Phillip's Lake area
7	Wild and scenic rivers (scenic portions only)
11	HCNRA dispersed recreation/timber management
17	Utility corridors
18	Anadromous fish emphasis

Chapter 3: Vegetation Management on National Forest Lands Since 1988

William McArthur, Gary Lettman, David Powell, Victoria Rockwell, and Edward Uebler

Introduction

To provide an historical context, former Oregon Governor Kitzhaber requested an overview of management actions that have occurred over at least the past decade. Various and often conflicting perspectives exist on the intensity and impact of management activities that have occurred in the recent past. We reviewed historical management records to provide objective information on how much land has been affected by management over the past decade and to assess the extent to which this management has influenced exiting conditions.

Methods

The TRACS-SILVA records stored at the U.S. Department of Agriculture's National Computer Center in Kansas City were used to determine the area of national forest land affected by commercial timber harvest, noncommercial thinning (forest density management), and reforestation annually from 1988 until 2001. Wildfire acres were derived from geographic information system layers at each national forest office. Oregon Department of Forestry timber harvest reports were used to determine timber harvest volumes from national forest lands in Baker, Grant, Harney, Malheur, Umatilla, Union, Wallowa, and Wheeler Counties from 1980 until 2000.

Results

Table 3-1 displays the area of national forest lands affected by timber harvest, noncommercial thinning, wildfire, and reforestation from 1988 to 2001. During the 14-year period, conditions on 1.2 million acres were altered by vegetation management and wildfire. Timber harvest occurred on approximately 480,000 acres. Over 245,000 acres were precommercially thinned (i.e., trees removed lacked commercial value). Wildfires burned over 611,000 acres.

Since 1980, average annual timber harvest from national forest lands has ranged from 68 to over 672 million board feet (MMBF) (fig. 3-1). Harvest peaked between 1985 and 1992, when annual outputs exceeded 500 MMBF. Since 1997, timber harvest has declined to less than 100 MMBF per year.

Table 3-1—Vegetation management on the Blue Mountains national forests

	1988	1989	1990	1991	1992	1993	1994	1995	1996	1997	1998	1999	2000	2001	Total
							Acres								
Timber harvest:															
Clearcut	5,857	7,145	13,856	8,921	7,777	5,265	1,453	1,181	1,164	2,855	1,740	1,418	0	109	58,741
Prep cut	515	0	171	370	614	179	182	0	161	0	99	48	0	0	2,339
Seed cut	11,912	9,179	17,502	8,051	9,086	8,491	12,550	5,972	3,570	5,578	3,243	3,443	2,464	249	101,290
Removal cut	12,450	16,299	27,592	24,159	23,406	13,291	16,529	4,775	1,142	58	1,192	199	691	116	141,899
Selection cut	4,732	274	2,331	1,718	2,101	2,736	1,492	2,201	1,091	3,922	1,486	4,108	1,428	1,420	31,040
Improvement cut	0	0	0	0	74	168	0	0	209	564	349	99	368	1,340	3,171
Thinning cut	623	274	5,136	1,113	3,319	2,447	3,522	3,289	1,978	6,403	8,774	12,101	7,069	6,641	62,689
Sanitation cut	945	629	12,166	3,672	7,064	15,020	1,541	2,004	3,651	16,182	3,267	9,090	1,900	1,736	78,867
Special cut	396	914	0	0	5	16	56	519	128	381	92	24	0	127	2,658
Total harvest	37,430	34,714	78,754	48,004	53,446	47,613	37,325	19,941	13,094	35,943	20,242	30,530	13,920	11,738	482,694
Density management:															
Release[a]	1,510	1,087	2,404	2,049	2,527	1,885	445	364	5	136	116	300	390	0	13,218
Precommercial thinning	15,666	16,986	15,672	16,929	16,832	17,469	17,401	17,259	20,331	17,893	15,073	11,992	11,215	21,691	232,409
Total thinning	17,176	18,073	18,076	18,978	19,359	19,354	17,846	17,623	20,336	18,029	15,189	12,292	11,605	21,691	245,627
Other changes:															
Wildfires (>100 acres)	61,462	76,602	32,103	612	3,611	470	96,613	2,906	214,662	3,742	680	640	100,380	16,753	611,236
Reforestation	16,528	19,882	20,766	23,968	29,661	33,533	42,021	30,186	33,938	25,221	26,900	19,965	17,248	11,802	351,619
Total other	77,990	96,484	52,869	24,580	33,272	34,003	138,634	33,092	248,600	28,963	27,580	20,605	117,628	28,555	962,855

[a] Noncommercial removal of larger trees that are inhibiting the growth of smaller but more desirable species.

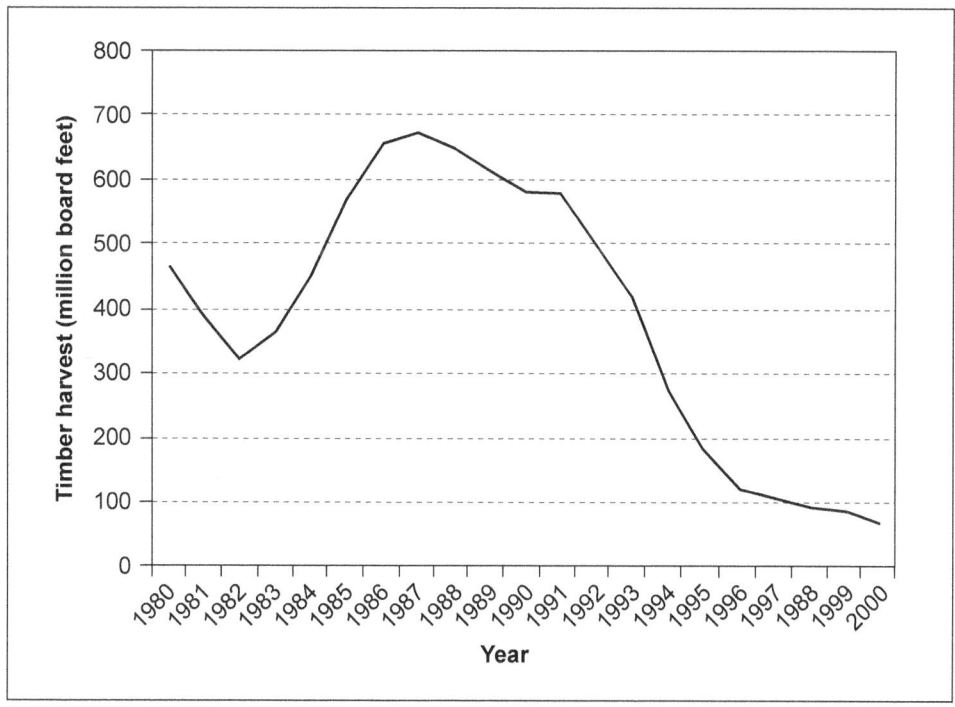

Figure 3-1—National forest harvests in Baker, Grant, Harney, Union, Wallowa, and Wheeler Counties (3-year moving average). (From: Oregon Department of Forestry annual timber harvest reports).

Discussion

Over the 14 years prior to this analysis, about 30 percent of the 1.6 million acres of national forest land available for active harvest underwent some sort of timber harvest (Braymen et al. this volume). Some of these acres were probably counted more than once in annual reports because more than one type of silvicultural treatment and harvest likely occurred during the 14-year period of record.

Because of high insect-induced mortality, most commercially harvested stands were treated by using seed-tree cuts or clearcuts. With clearcuts, all trees in a stand are harvested in one operation. Only "leave" trees for snag recruitment and riparian buffers were unharvested. Under seed-tree harvests, all trees are harvested in one operation except for a few seed-producing trees left to regenerate the stand. Those seed trees are harvested with removal cuts after the stand has sufficiently regenerated. Seed tree and removal cuts were the predominant methods used to treat stands commercially during this period. Clearcuts were used when no suitable seed trees existed.

Selective harvest techniques that cut individual trees, such as sanitation or commercial thinning cuts, were also used, but on a smaller percentage of the area. Together individual-tree harvest techniques over the period accounted for about 173,000 acres or about 36 percent of the acreage treated commercially.

The type of harvest also changed considerably during the 14 years prior to this analysis (fig. 3-2). From 1988 until about 1995, clearcuts, seed-tree harvests, and removal harvests were the most common commercial harvest techniques, generally accounting for over 60 percent of the acreage treated commercially. After 1995, use of these treatments dropped off precipitously. For all years after 1997, they accounted for less than 30 percent of the harvested area—dropping to 10 percent in 2000 and 2001. In contrast, commercial thinning shows almost the opposite pattern: it increased from less than 10 percent of the area treated in 1988 through 1994 to more than 50 percent of the area treated by the end of the preanalysis period. The other two major harvest methods (sanitation cuts and selection cuts) were more variable and less frequently used.

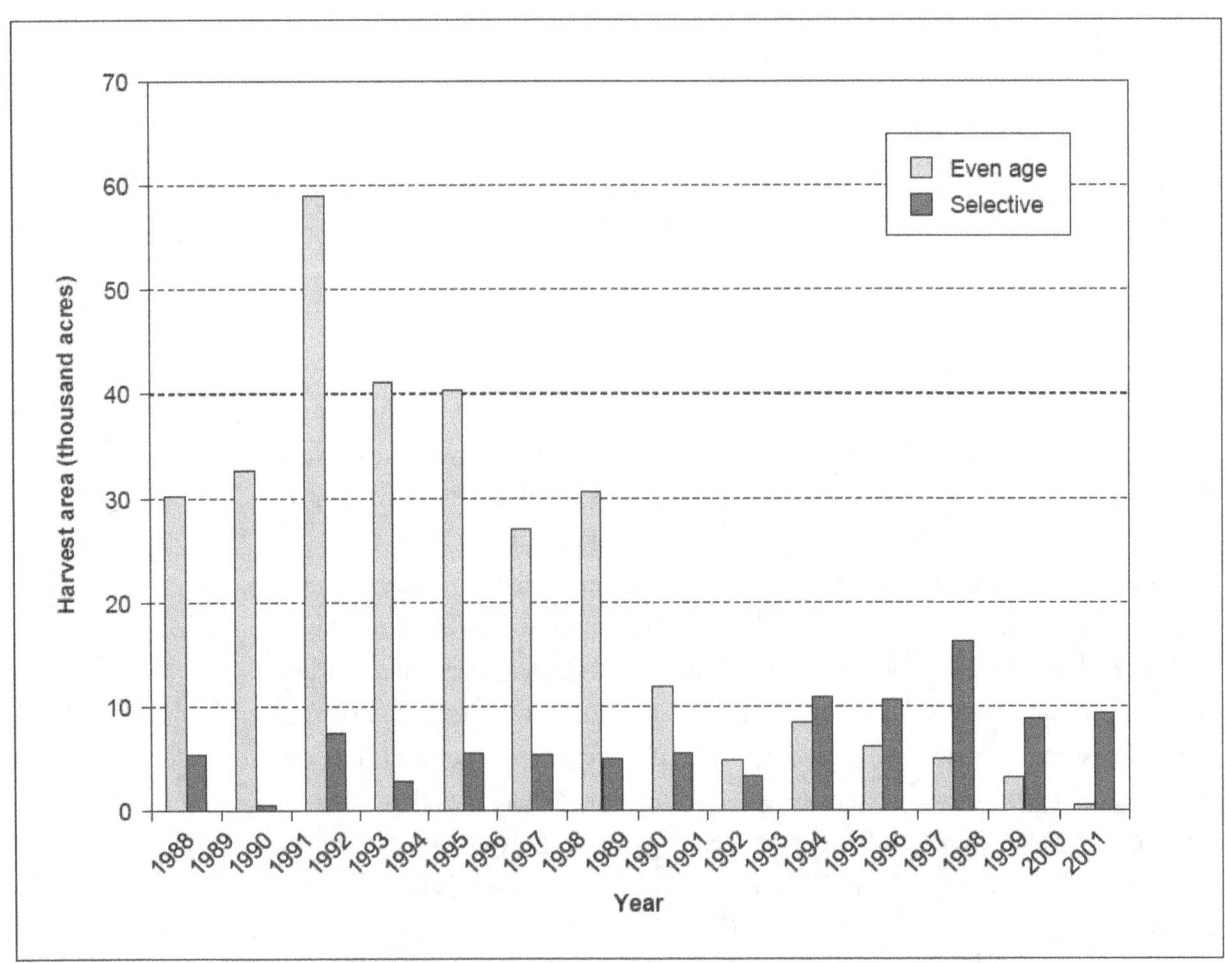

Figure 3-2—Acres of even-age (clearcuts and seed tree) harvests and selective (individual-tree) harvest on the national forests from 1988 to 2001.

Precommercial thinning was the final major vegetation management method practiced prior to this analysis. Nearly a quarter million acres were precommercially thinned during this period. The rate was relatively constant with about 15,000 acres being treated in each year (table 3-1). This may be related to funding levels appropriated by the U.S. Congress rather than resource need. In other words, it is likely that more acres were in need of thinning than were actually thinned.

This analysis and the information presented by Rainville (this volume) on insect outbreaks in the Blue Mountains suggest that on average, wildfire and insects affect many more acres each year than does timber harvest. Although our analysis does not compare the exact outcomes of wildfire and insect outbreaks, it is probably fair to say that they each had an effect on the structure and composition of the remaining vegetation. In some cases, nearly all of the trees died, whereas in others only scattered individual trees were killed. In all cases, where openings were created by any means—e.g., wildfire, insect attack, or timber harvest—dense regeneration likely followed. In the absence of active management or low-intensity wildfires, these stands will remain dense for many decades, perhaps even centuries. Trees growing in these openings will not obtain large size, and open single-storied stands will not tend to develop over much of the landscape (Hemstrom et al. 2007). When cattle, deer, and elk grazing are added to the equation, even higher levels of small trees can be expected (Vavra et al. 2007).

On average, wildfire and insects affect many more acres each year than does timber harvest.

Conclusions

Since 1988, timber harvest and precommercial thinning have occurred on up to 587,000 acres (32 percent) of the area in the active forestry and lynx management area categories (MACs). Based on our knowledge of standard practice on these forests, we assumed that little timber harvest or thinning was conducted in riparian zones, roadless areas, old-growth areas, or on lands within the reserved MACs. We also assumed that the total acreage affected by timber harvest is equal to the "total timber harvest" acres minus "removal cut" acres in table 3-1, and that "removal cut" harvests occurred on the same acres reported as "clearcut" or "seed cut."

Based on these assumptions, we conclude that regenerating stands located in many of the areas harvested since 1988 have matured into densely stocked[1] conditions where thinning treatments will primarily yield small, noncommercial timber. Past experience suggests that funding will be needed to accomplish these treatments.

---

[1] Densely stocked stands are defined here as stands with stocking of greater than 45 percent of the maximum stand density index or more than 300 trees per acre smaller than 4 inches at breast height.

Metric Equivalents

When you know:	Multiply by:	To find:
Inches	2.54	Centimeters
Acres	.405	Hectares
Million board feet (MMBF)	5.67	Thousand cubic meters

Literature Cited

Hemstrom, M.; Merzenich, J.; Reger, A.; Wales, B. 2007. Integrated analysis of landscape management scenarios using state and transition models in the upper Grande Ronde River subbasin, Oregon, USA. Landscape and Urban Planning. 80: 198–211.

Vavra, M.; Hemstrom, M.; Wisdom, M. 2007. Modeling the effects of herbivores on the abundance of forest overstory states using a state-transition approach in the upper Grande Ronde River basin, Oregon, USA. Landscape and Urban Planning. 80: 212–222.

Chapter 4: The Quantity, Composition, and Economic Value of Timber Resulting From Treating Densely Stocked[1] Stands Within Areas Suitable for Sustainable Harvest

Jamie Barbour, Bruce Countryman, Roger Fight, Donald Justice, William McArthur, David Powell, Victoria Rockwell, Ryan Singleton, and Edward Uebler

Introduction

The economies of many communities in the Blue Mountains have traditionally depended on forest products. As a result, the economic impact of forestry activities on national forests is important to the people who live there. A large-scale thinning program might benefit communities by providing employment in the woods, and if sufficient quantities of commercially valued timber could be harvested and transported at costs less than the market value of the wood, manufacturing jobs would also result.

The economic outcome of forestry management activities is also important to federal land managers. Where restoration treatments are financially feasible, managers are better able to treat high-priority resource areas. They can implement needed stand thinning without reliance on financial subsidies or use of stewardship contracting, in which thinning of areas with positive net revenues is used to offset thinning costs in areas with negative net revenues.

Management's ability to implement prescriptions designed to increase the resilience of federally administered forests to natural and human-caused disturbances may be inhibited by economic limitations even with stewardship management authorities. Stands treated with restoration prescriptions may not provide financially viable timber sales. For example, if the objective is to restore pre-Euro-American settlement stand conditions, economic outcomes may be seen as secondary to residual stand structure objectives. Generally, higher valued large trees are maintained preferentially. Species are selected for harvest based upon site suitability without regard to their market value. Harvest volumes and locations are based on management's desire to create a certain residual stand condition rather than to achieve socioeconomic objectives. These treatments may call for the harvest of high volumes of low-value timber products or of small volumes of potentially valuable timber that is widely dispersed. Thinning operations may not be financially viable.

> **Management's ability to implement prescriptions designed to increase the resilience of federally administered forests may be inhibited by economic limitations even with stewardship management authorities.**

[1] Densely stocked stands are defined here as stands with stocking of greater than 45 percent of the maximum stand density index or more than 300 trees per acre smaller than 4 inches at breast height.

Methods

Forest Service Continuous Vegetation Survey (CVS) data were used to estimate volumes and characteristics of timber resulting from thinning of densely stocked stands in the active forestry management category (MAC) defined in chapter 2. The CVS inventory system is described at http://www.fs.fed.us/r6/survey. The CVS plot data collected from 1994 to 2001 were used. Only inventory plots that fell within the active forestry MAC were analyzed. Plots within nonforest plant associations or that met the Forest Service Pacific Northwest Region's definition of late- and old-forest structure were removed from the analysis.

Tree growth on the active forestry MAC plots was projected forward to 2002 by using the Forest Service Forest Vegetation Simulator (FVS) (Crookston and Dixon 2005). The FVS is a distance-independent individual-tree-growth-and-yield model that aggregates results on a per-acre basis.

Stand density index (SDI) (Cochran et al. 1994, Powell 1999) provides a measure of each stand's site potential, and was used to identify densely stocked stands. Densely stocked conditions were assumed if the SDI of a plot met one or more of the following conditions:

1. If stand density was more than 45 percent of the maximum SDI (fig. 4-1a) for the plot's plant association, the stand was thinned to 35 percent of the maximum SDI.

2. If stand density was less than 45 percent of the maximum SDI (fig. 4-1b) but there were more than 300 trees per acre (TPA) with diameters ranging from 0.1 to 7 inches diameter at breast height (d.b.h), the stand was thinned to 135 TPA (approximately 18 feet between trees).

Cochran et al. (1994) and Powell (1999) were used to determine the desired stand density after thinning. To simulate a thin-from-below prescription, the FVS prescription preferentially removed smaller trees to achieve the desired density. Exceptions to the general rule of preserving the largest trees occurred if larger trees were severely mistletoe-infected or seriously damaged, or if multiple species were present with larger trees that were not the site's preferred species of ponderosa pine (*Pinus ponderosa* P. & C. Lawson), western larch (*Larix occidentalis* Nutt.), or western white pine (*Pinus monticola* Dougl. ex D. Don). All trees larger than 21 inches d.b.h. were preserved without consideration of tree health, tree damage, or species preferences, to incorporate the Regional Forester's Forest Plan Amendment 2 harvest restrictions (commonly known as the east-side screens). However, the amendment does make exceptions for ecosystem benefit on occasion, such as allowing for removal of white fir (*Abies concolor* Gord. & Glend.).

USDA Forest Service, Pacific Northwest Region

USDA Forest Service, Pacific Northwest Region

Figure 4-1—Comparison of (a) a densely stocked stand and (b) a stand stocked at a density of less than 45 percent of maximum stand density index.

The FVS model produced information for each tree harvested on each plot. The model's outputs were summarized according to tree species, diameter classes, county, forest, aspect, slope, and other plot attributes.

Financial outcomes were estimated by using the Financial Analysis of Ecosystem Management Activities model (FEEMA) (Fight and Chmelik 1998). The analysis compared the value of timber products produced at a mill to the costs of contracting, harvesting, and transporting the timber.

The value per cubic foot (CF) for each log species group was estimated by averaging product prices for the fourth quarter of 1999 and the fourth quarter of 2001. Product values were determined for each species group based upon the small-end diameter of the log (table 4-1). Value estimates are regional averages that do not reflect local variations in bid prices that can occur.

Table 4-1—Assumed dollar value of logs delivered to a mill

Small-end diameter	Douglas-fir and larch	Hemlock, grand fir, and Engelmann spruce	Ponderosa pine	Lodgepole pine
Inches	------------- *Dollars per hundred cubic feet* -------------			
4	1	1	1	1
6	90	58	11	43
7	143	106	84	100
10	186	144	155	142
13	210	166	206	163
16	225	180	248	173
19	236	190	284	178

Harvest costs (dollars per hundred cubic feet [CCF]) for each stand were estimated based on log size and the number of trees harvested per acre (tables 4-2 and 4-3). Cable-based yarding systems were assumed on slopes greater than 35 percent.

The following tabulation shows the operation costs assuming average conditions:

Activity	Dollars per CCF
Hauling	27
Road maintenance	7
Contractual requirements	9
Temporary roads	1
Specified roads	0
Required reforestation	0

Table 4-2—Assumed ground-based harvest costs

Tree size	Number of cut trees per acre					
	5	20	50	100	200	400
Cubic feet per cut tree	*- - - - - - Dollars per hundred cubic feet - - - - -*					
3					104	97
5				85	78	73
10			67	61	57	54
50		41	38	38	36	36
100	38	38	38	38	36	35
150	37	37	37	37	36	35

Table 4-3—Assumed cable-based harvest costs

Tree size	Number of cut trees per acre					
	5	20	50	100	200	400
Cubic feet per cut tree	*- - - - - - Dollars per hundred cubic feet - - - - - -*					
3					368	257
5				385	232	178
10			296	207	141	119
50		86	82	75	73	72
100	71	59	57	57	56	56
150	57	55	54	54	54	54

When log values exceeded total operation costs, the thinning treatment had a positive net revenue and could be accomplished without the need for additional funding to offset costs. When operation costs exceeded log values, the treatment had a negative net revenue and could not be accomplished without additional funding.

The study's estimates of densely stocked acres and the harvested timber's size, species composition, commercial value, and maximum volumes describe outcomes on a landscape scale across the entire Blue Mountains province. Localized county results are reported because of local interest. Reliability of localized estimates is subject to the following considerations.

- Only a small number of sample plots were available in some counties. In these situations, the limited sample size may not accurately represent over-all county conditions.

- Management concerns such as cumulative effects on wildlife and aquatic resources, soil and visual sensitivity, and operational feasibility could not be assessed at the scale of this report. As a result, the estimates of acres available for treatment and quantities of timber resulting from thinning likely exceed attainable levels and should be viewed as upper limits.

• The analysis is based on application of a generalized thinning prescription and regional economic data. Changes in the prescription and economic assumptions to account for local vegetation management needs, operational capabilities, markets, and competition would alter the results.

Results

The analysis indicated that up to 943,000 acres (58 percent) of national forest lands in the active forestry timber availability category are densely stocked (table 4-4).

Table 4-4—Densely stocked acres on national forests within each county

County	Densely stocked national forest land		Densely stocked area yielding < 400 CF per acre of merchantable timber		Densely stocked area yielding ≥ 400 CF per acre of merchantable timber	
	Thousand acres	Number of plots	Thousand acres	Number of plots	Thousand acres	Number of plots
Baker	113	88	42	32	71 ± 4^a	56
Grant	391	260	188	123	203 ± 9	137
Harney	167	117	90	61	77 ± 5	56
Morrow	51	26	33	17	18 ± 3	9
Umatilla	58	35	38	24	20 ± 5	11
Union	89	77	45	38	44 ± 6	39
Wallowa	49	41	22	19	27 ± 6	22
Crook and Wheeler	25	14	12	7	13 ± 2	7
Totals	943	572	472	235	471 ± 16	337

Note: CF = cubic feet.
[a] 95-percent confidence limit.

Simulations showed that thinning would yield less than 400 CF of merchantable timber per acre on nearly half of the acreage (472,000 acres) (fig. 4-2). These low yields would be inadequate to support a commercially viable treatment, so the economic potential of these acres was not evaluated.

If thinning of densely stocked stands was financially feasible and consistent with site-specific constraints, 1,517 million board feet (MMBF) of timber could be harvested from the stands (fig. 4-3), yielding greater than 400 CF of merchantable material per acre (table 4-5). The gross volume available would be 425 million cubic feet (MMCF).

Figure 4-2—A densely stocked stand where thinning would yield less than 400 cubic feet of merchantable timber.

Figure 4-3—Typical densely stocked stand that will yield small-diameter timber when thinned.

Table 4-5—Potential saw-log and gross volumes from densely stocked national forest stands yielding 400 cubic feet per acre or more

County	Potential saw-log volume	Potential gross cubic foot volume
	Million board feet	*Thousand cubic feet*
Baker	236 ± 31[a]	61 ± 6
Grant	590 ± 45	174 ± 12
Harney	200 ± 21	60 ± 6
Morrow	68 ± 23	18 ± 6
Umatilla	73 ± 24	20 ± 6
Union	143 ± 48	39 ± 6
Wallowa	128 ± 36	32 ± 11
Crook and Wheeler	7 ± 836	22 ± 9
Totals	1,517 ± 95	425 ± 24

[a] 95-percent confidence limit.

Simulated thinning of densely stocked stands with potential yields greater than 400 CF per acre generated relatively low volumes per acre. Almost 40 percent of the volume was composed of trees smaller than 10 inches d.b.h., and 67 percent were trees smaller than 13 inches d.b.h. Trees larger than 16 inches d.b.h. accounted for less than 15 percent of the harvest volume. Harvest volumes averaged 3,200 BF per acre (table 4-6). Small Douglas-fir (*Pseudotsuga menziesii* (Mirb.) Franco), grand fir (*Abies grandis* Dougl. ex D. Don), and ponderosa pine trees (tables 4-6 and 4-7) made up much of the harvested volume.

Commercial thinning would only be possible where the value of the timber harvested exceeds the cost of the harvesting, hauling, road maintenance, and contractual requirements (i.e., a positive net revenue exists). Because most simulated thinnings harvested low volumes of small trees, commercial removal was possible on only 39,900 (± 4,600) acres, or less than 10 percent of the densely stocked acres (table 4-8). The saw-log volume harvested totaled 167 (± 36) MMBF. The gross volume was 41 (± 8) MMCF.

Figure 4-4 compares the total densely stocked acres in each county to the acres with a positive net revenue.

Financial analysis indicated that most densely stocked stands could not be thinned without some investment. Up to $250 per acre would be needed to treat 136,000 acres (fig. 4-5). Another 138,000 acres could be treated for $250 to $500 per acre. Figure 4-6 distributes densely stocked acres within each county into net revenue classes.

Because most simulated thinnings harvested low volumes of small trees, commercial removal was possible on less than 10 percent of the densely stocked acres

Most densely stocked stands could not be thinned without some investment.

Table 4-6—Average harvest volume per acre resulting from thinning of stands yielding 400 cubic feet per acre or more

Diameter class	Average volume per acre	Percentage of total
Inches	*Board feet*	*Percent*
<7	103	3
7 to 10	1,134	35
10 to 13	916	28
13 to 16	607	19
>16	456	14
Total	3,216	

Table 4-7—Saw-log volume by species group

County	Douglas-fir	Grand fir	Ponderosa pine	Lodgepole pine	Juniper	Larch	Alpine fir, Engelmann spruce
				Percent			
Baker	41	19	26	6	4	2	2
Grant	34	26	20	14	4	2	0
Harney	25	17	49	0	9	0	0
Morrow	44	17	7	15	1	11	5
Umatilla	29	28	0	34	0	1	8
Union	40	23	4	22	0	8	2
Wallowa	38	24	4	16	0	10	9
Crook and Wheeler	41	21	26	0	2	3	6
Total	35	23	22	12	4	3	2

Table 4-8—Number of densely stocked acres and timber volume where thinning would result in a positive net value

County	Densely stocked areas with a positive net value	Saw-log volume with a positive net value	Gross volume with a positive net value
	Thousand acres	*Million board feet*	*Million cubic feet*
Baker	9.6 ± 1.8[a]	49 ± 16	11 ± 4
Grant	11.2 ± 2.6	42 ± 13	10 ± 3
Harney	8.9 ± 2.5	27 ± 12	8 ± 3
Morrow	1.0 —	3 —	1 —
Umatilla	0	0	0
Union	4.1 ± 2.6	14 ± 8	3 ± 2
Wallowa	2.4 —	21 —	5 —
Crook and Wheeler	2.7 ± 4.8	10 ± 4	3 ± 2
Totals	39.9 ± 4.6	167 ± 36	41 ± 8

— Indicates that no confidence limits could be estimated because only one plot was available.

[a] 95-percent confidence limit.

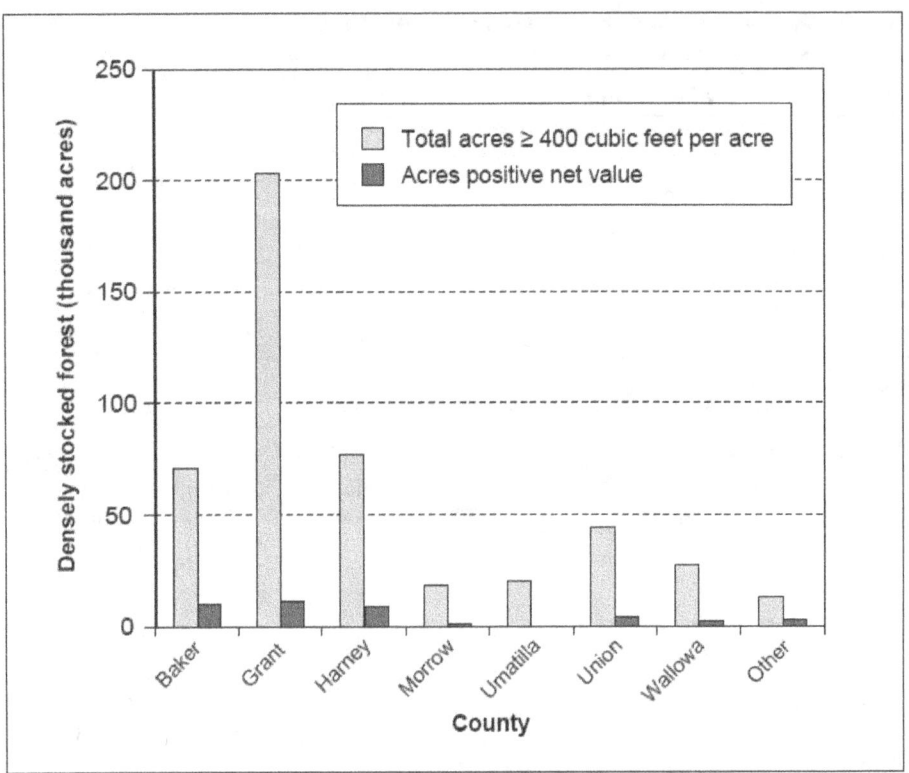

Figure 4-4—Total densely stocked acres with yields 400 cubic feet or more per acre compared to acres with positive net value for each county.

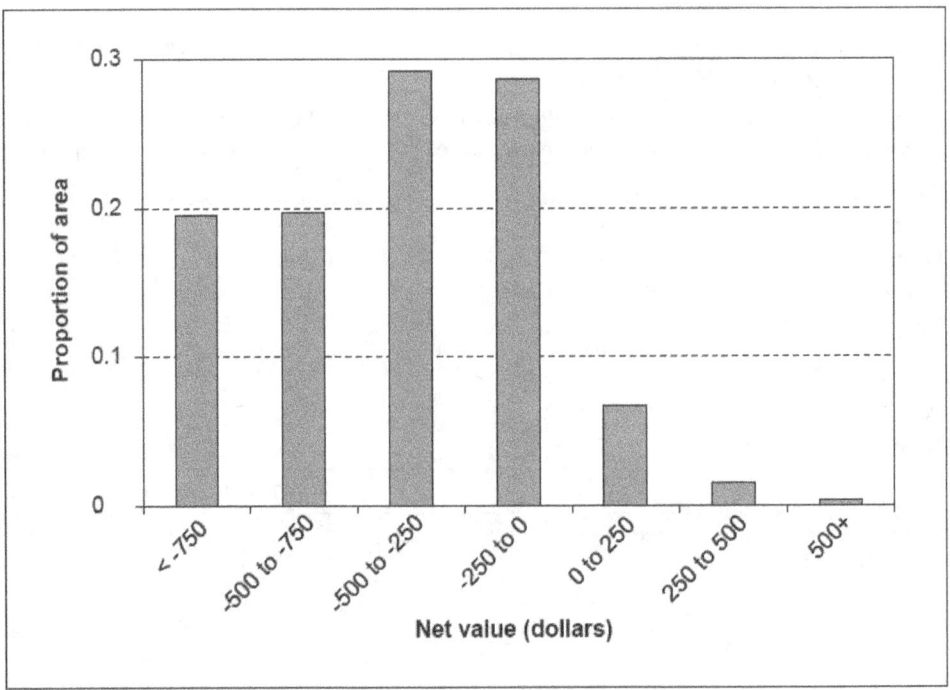

Figure 4-5—Distribution of economic net values associated with thinning of densely stocked area in the active forestry category.

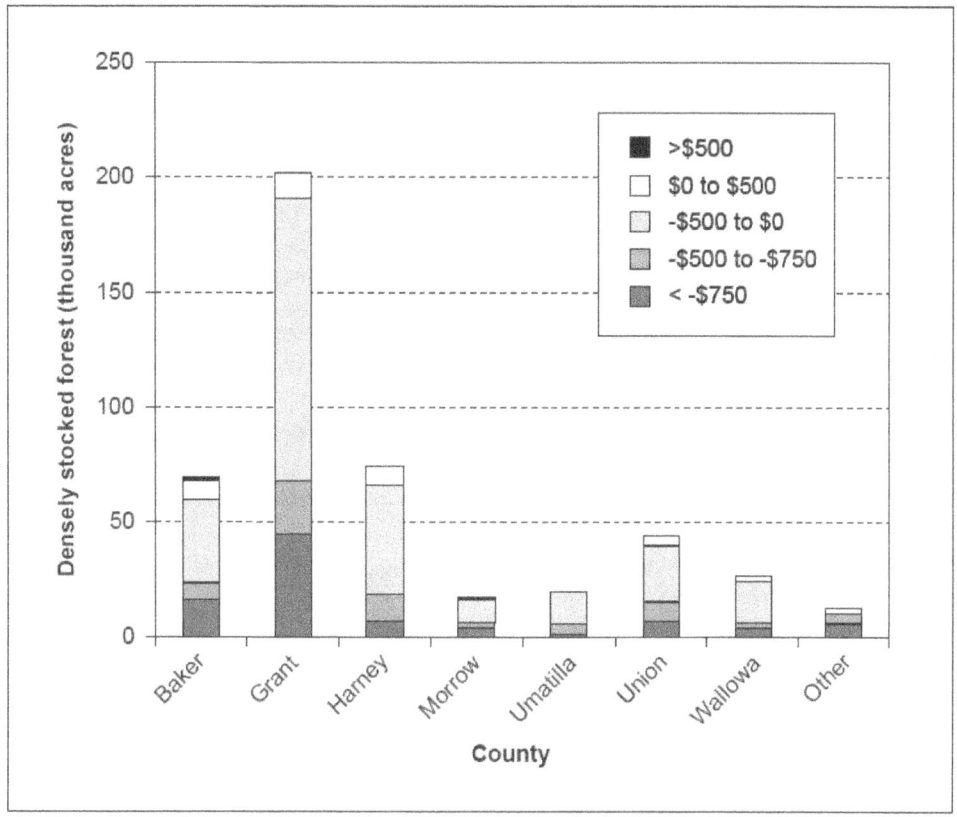

Figure 4-6—Area of densely stocked stands by county and distribution of net values associated with thinning.

Conclusions

Although the analysis estimated that 58 percent (943,000 acres) of the active forestry MAC lands were densely stocked, thinning of these lands will be limited by the low value of the timber harvested and the high costs of harvest, transportation, and manufacturing (fig. 4-7). Many of the densely stocked acres were likely treated within the past 30 years. As a result, thinning of 472,000 acres yielded only incidental amounts of merchantable timber (less than 400 cubic feet per acre).

When a thinning prescription was simulated on the remaining 471,000 acres, most (66 percent) of the trees harvested were less than 13 inches d.b.h., and the average quantity of timber removed was 3,200 board feet (BF)/acre. High operational costs and low market values associated with harvest of such low volumes of small trees would undermine the potential for commercial treatments on most densely stocked acres. The industry that existed in the Blue Mountains prior to the early 1990s was primarily focused on processing mid-sized to large logs (>15 inches in diameter). Use of materials from thinning densely stocked stands will require the development of new markets for a different set of products (Barbour and Skog 1997).

High operational costs and low market values associated with harvest of such low volumes of small trees would undermine the potential for commercial treatments on most densely stocked acres.

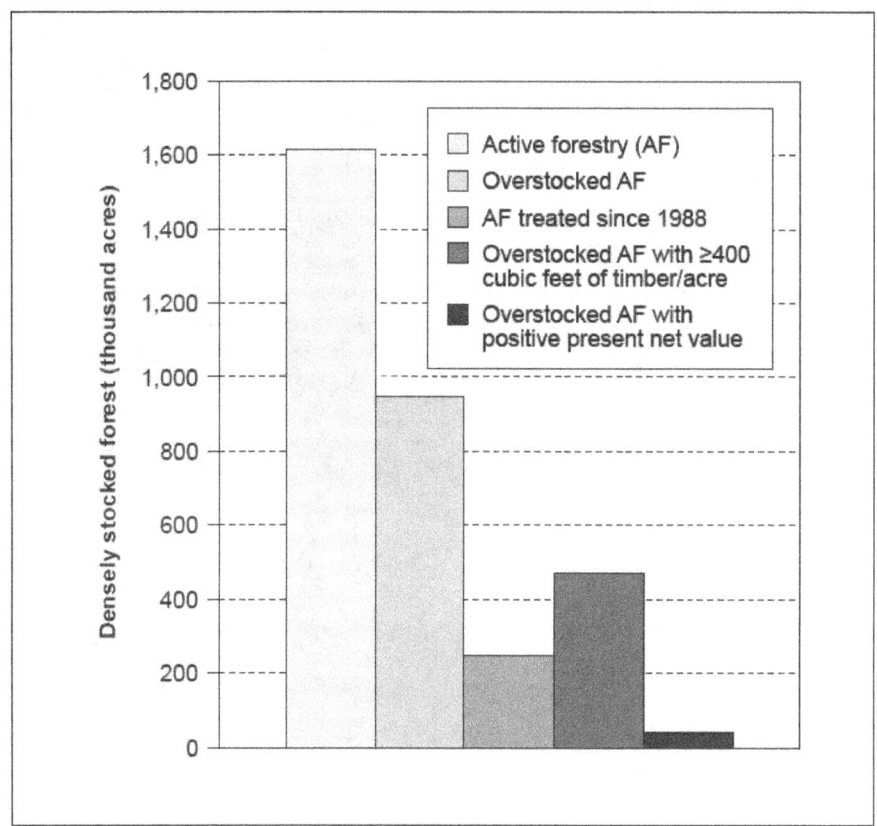

Figure 4-7—Potential for commercial thinning of densely stocked lands on national forests.

Based on this analysis, thinning had a positive net revenue on only 39,900 acres (± 4,600). Another 136,000 acres had borderline commercial potential where thinning could be accomplished with investments of less than $250 per acre. For $250 to $500 per acre, management could thin 138,000 more acres. Changes in market values, industrial demand, availability of subsidies, or agency policies could make thinning commercially viable on many of these densely stocked acres. Nevertheless, even when considered under the most favorable of assumptions, most densely stocked stands would not be treatable without significant investments.

This report raises important questions about the role of the Forest Service in keeping the timber industry and allied communities healthy. For one thing, what is the demand for national forest timber, and how does it change under different futures? How competitive is the Blue Mountains timber industry relative to other regions? In thinking about the future of the timber industry in this region, it may be useful to consider whether national forests can make a difference.

Species list

Douglas-fir	*Pseudotsuga menziesii* (Mirb.) Franco
Larch	*Larix* spp
Hemlock	*Tsuga* spp.
Grand fir	*Abies grandis* Dougl. ex D. Don
Engelmann spruce	*Picea engelmannii* Parry ex Engelm
Ponderosa pine	*Pinus ponderosa* P. & C. Lawson
Lodgepole pine	*Pinus contorta* Dougl. ex Loud

Metric Equivalents

When you know:	Multiply by:	To find:
Inches	2.54	Centimeters
Feet	.305	Meters
Cubic feet (CF)	.0283	Cubic meters
Acres	.405	Hectares
Million board feet (MMBF)	5.67	Thousand cubic meters
Trees per acre	2.47	Trees per hectare

Literature Cited

Barbour, R.J.; Skog, K.E., eds. 1997. Role of wood production in ecosystem management: proceedings of the Sustainable Forestry Working Group at the IUFRO all division 5 conference. Gen. Tech. Rep. FPL-GTR-100. Madison, WI: U.S. Department of Agriculture, Forest Service, Forest Products Laboratory.

Cochran, P.H.; Geist, J.M.; Clemens, D.L.; Clausnitzer, R.; Powell, D.C. 1994. Suggested stocking levels for forest stands in northeastern Oregon and southeastern Washington. Res. Note PNW-RN-513. Portland, OR: U.S. Department of Agriculture, Forest Service, Pacific Northwest Research Station. 26 p.

Crookston, N.L.; Dixon, G.E. 2005. The Forest Vegetation Simulator: a review of its structure, content, and applications. Computers and Electronics in Agriculture. 49: 60–80.

Fight, R.D.; Chmelik, J.T. 1998. Analysts guide to FEEMA for financial analysis of ecosystem management activities. Gen. Tech. Rep. FPL-GTR-111. Madison, WI: U.S. Department of Agriculture, Forest Service, Forest Products Laboratory. 5 p.

Powell, D.C. 1999. Suggested stocking levels for forest stands in northeastern Oregon and southeastern Washington: an implementation guide for the Umatilla National Forest. F14-SO-TP-03-1999. Pendleton, OR: U.S. Department of Agriculture, Forest Service, Pacific Northwest Region, Umatilla National Forest. 72 p.

Chapter 5: The Effect of New and Proposed Policy Changes on Managers' Ability to Thin Densely Stocked[1] Stands and Reduce Fire Risk

Jamie Barbour, Bruce Countryman, Roger Fight, Donald Justice, William McArthur, David Powell, Victoria Rockwell, Ryan Singleton, and Edward Uebler

Introduction

In 1994, the regional forester in the Pacific Northwest Region amended forest plans by adding a requirement prohibiting harvest of live trees larger than 21 inches diameter at breast height (d.b.h.). The amendment is applied regardless of tree health or species preference for the site. The policy was intended to maintain habitat options for species associated with east-side old-growth forests. The requirement has been controversial because larger trees generally have higher value and can be harvested and transported more efficiently than smaller trees. Critics have speculated that many more acres of densely stocked stands could be treated profitably if the requirement were eliminated and managers were freed to harvest large trees that were unhealthy or inappropriate for the site.

Another policy change came in 2003. Through this change, Congress provided the Forest Service with the ability to use receipts collected from profitable thinning treatments to accomplish thinnings or other management activities in which the market value of the timber removed is less than implementation costs (Section 323 of Public Law 108-7). Prior to this law, managers were required to treat profit-generating harvests separately from nonprofitable treatments. Two separate contracts were needed. In addition, receipts generated from profitable thinnings were returned to the U.S. Treasury and were not available for silvicultural treatments outside the treatment area. The new legislation enabled an administrative tool that has come to be known as stewardship contracting. With stewardship contracting, managers can combine profit-generating thinnings and nonprofitable treatments in one contract. Funds generated from profitable treatments can be used to, among other things, treat densely stocked stands in which treatment costs exceed the value of the harvested timber.

This analysis evaluated some of the consequences of these two policy changes: stewardship contracting and eliminating the 21-inch upper diameter limit on timber removals from land administered by the USDA Forest Service in eastern Oregon.

> **This analysis evaluated some of the consequences of stewardship contracting and the 21-inch upper diameter limit on timber removals.**

---

[1] Densely stocked stands are defined here as stands with stocking of greater than 45 percent of the maximum stand density index or more than 300 trees per acre smaller than 4 inches at breast height.

Former Oregon Governor Kitzhaber requested that this analysis estimate the potential benefits of these new policies because they had been identified as changes that could enhance restoration work. This analysis provides a broad-scale assessment. Different modeling techniques (cf Wales et al. 2007) or site-specific surveys or analyses would be needed to account for more site-specific resource needs, such as wildlife snag habitat.

Methods

The effect of new authorities allowing reinvestment of receipts was evaluated by performing the analysis described in chapter 3. Receipts derived from treatments with positive net revenues (where net revenue equals the revenue from the sale of timber minus all treatment and transportation costs) were used to pay the costs needed to accomplish treatments with negative net revenues. The least negative net revenue stands were treated first. The resulting increase in acres treated was tallied and compared to the total with no reinvestment.

To estimate the effect of the regional forester's amendment (commonly known as the east-side screens), two analyses were made using the process described in chapter 3. The first analysis limited harvest to trees less than 21 inches d.b.h. to simulate outcomes associated with the amendment. The second removed the 21-inch restriction and allowed the harvest of trees that were diseased, damaged, or undesirable for the site. Increases in treatment acres having positive economic values were attributed to managers' ability to harvest larger trees when the restriction was removed.

Results

Effect of Reinvestment of Harvest Receipts From Stands With Positive Net Revenues

The assessment found that an additional 75,000 acres could be thinned, and 225 million board feet (MMBF) of saw logs could be harvested commercially if national forests were able to reinvest receipts from the thinning of stands with positive net revenues to treat those with negative net revenues (table 5-1). This analysis considered only the costs of removing the densely stocked merchantable trees. In some cases, additional expenses would be required to treat nonmerchantable material to meet fire-hazard reduction or insect and disease objectives.

Table 5-1—The effect of reinvesting receipts from thinning stands with positive net values to treat those with negative net values

Scenario	Without reinvestment of receipts		With reinvestment of receipts	
	Treatable area	Volume harvested	Treatable area	Volume harvested
	Thousand acres	*Million board feet*	*Thousand acres*	*Million board feet*
With 21-inch d.b h. harvest limit (existing situation)	39.9	167	114.9	392
Without 21-inch d.b.h. harvest limit	79.1	356	223.1	807

D.b.h. = diameter at breast height.

Effect of Restriction on Harvesting Trees Larger Than 21 Inches Diameter at Breast Height

When the regional forester's forest plan amendment restriction on harvest of trees larger than 21 inches d.b.h. was removed, the number of densely stocked acres with positive net revenues nearly doubled, increasing from 39,900 to 79,100 acres. The saw-log volume with a positive net revenue increased from 167 (±36) MMBF to 356 (±57) MMBF (table 5-2).

Table 5-2—Densely stocked land with a positive net harvest value with and without restriction of harvest of trees larger than 21 inches diameter at breast height (d.b.h.)

County	With 21-inch d.b h. limitation		Without 21-inch d.b.h limitation	
	Area	Volume	Area	Volume
	Thousand acres	*Million board feet*	*Thousand acres*	*Million board feet*
Baker	9.6 ± 1.8[a]	49 ± 16	10.5 ± 1.9	58 ± 20
Grant	11.2 ± 2.6	42 ± 13	28.7 ± 3.4	121 ± 27
Harney	8.9 ± 2.5	27 ± 12	15.8 ± 2.6	54 ± 13
Morrow	1.0 —	3 —	4.3 ± 2.4	13 ± 7
Umatilla	0	0	2.4 —	16 —
Union	4.1 ± 2.6	14 ± 8	12.4 ± 2.3	51 ± 14
Wallowa	2.4 —	21 —	2.4 —	30 —
Crook and Wheeler	2.7 ± 4.8	10 ± 4	2.7 ± 4.8	13 ± 25
Totals	39.9 ± 4.6	167 ± 36	79.1 ± 5.7	356 ± 57

— Indicates that no confidence limits could be estimated because fewer than two plots were available for the county.
[a] 95-percent confidence limit.

To preserve trees larger than 21 inches d.b.h., the simulated prescription selected smaller healthy trees of desired species as needed to achieve the appropriate stand density. When this requirement was removed, the prescription was free to include harvest of larger trees if their species were not desired on the site or if they were damaged or diseased. As a result, harvest of trees larger than 16 inches d.b.h. increased from 456 to 750 BF per acre (table 5-3). Because larger trees command higher market prices and can be harvested more efficiently, thinning on an additional 39,000 acres had positive net revenues (table 5-2).

Table 5-3—Average harvest volumes per acre with and without a restriction on the harvest of trees larger than 21 inches diameter at breast height (d.b.h.)

Diameter class	With 21-inch d.b.h restriction		Without 21-inch d.b h. restriction	
Inches	*Board feet/acre*	*Percent*	*Board feet/acre*	*Percent*
<7	103	3	101	3
7 to 10	1,134	35	1,089	32
10 to 13	916	28	866	26
13 to 16	607	19	571	17
>16	456	14	750	22
Total	3,216		3,377	

When reinvestment of receipts was combined with the elimination of the restriction on harvest of trees larger than 21 inches d.b.h., the number of positive net value treatment acres increased by 144,000, yielding an additional 451 MMBF of saw logs (table 5-1).

Conclusions

Both the new and proposed policy changes evaluated here enhanced managers' ability to treat densely stocked stands cost-effectively. The modifications improved net economic results sufficiently to permit thinning of many of the 136,000 acres with borderline negative financial returns (chapter 3). Figure 5-1 compares the effectiveness of each policy modification in improving managers' ability to treat densely stocked stands.

Of the modifications, reinvestment of receipts yielded the most promising results. Often, negative net revenue stands are located close to positive net revenue treatments. Reinvestment of receipts improves managers' ability to treat more acres by providing funds needed to treat nearby negative net revenue stands. Although not evaluated in this assessment, reinvestment also improves overall operational

Reinvestment of receipts improves managers' ability to treat more acres by providing funds needed to treat nearby negative net revenue stands.

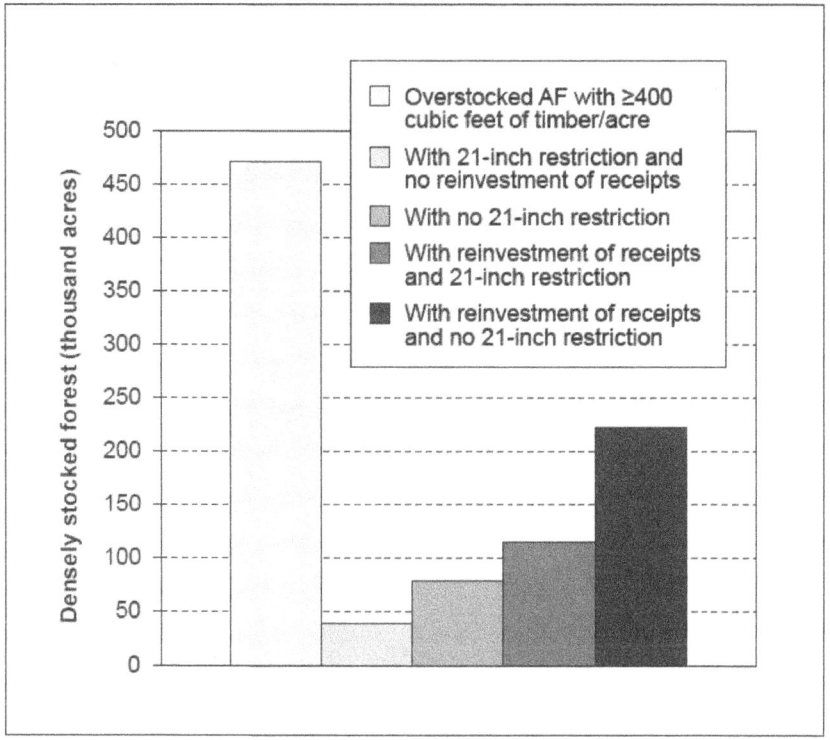

Figure 5-1—Effect of policy modifications on the number of densely stocked acres where thinning would result in a positive net value.

efficiency. Large areas can be treated with one project entry and with one contract. Duplication of administrative costs and some operational expenses such as move-in and move-out costs for logging equipment is avoided.

Elimination of the 21-inch d.b.h. harvest restriction also allowed thinning of more acres. This assessment did not, however, include considering the effects removing those large trees would have on other forest resources, such as snag-dependent wildlife. During project planning, habitat needs of animals that use large trees, and public input are considered. Consideration of these factors is likely to substantially reduce the number of acres and volume of large-diameter timber that would actually be harvested if the east-side screens were removed.

Metric Equivalents

When you know:	Multiply by:	To find:
Inches	2.54	Centimeters
Acres	.405	Hectares
Million board feet (MMBF)	5.67	Thousand cubic meters

Literature Cited

Wales, B.C.; Suring, L.H.; Hemstrom, M.A. 2007. Modeling potential outcomes of fire and fuel management scenarios on the structure of forested habitats in northeast Oregon, USA. Landscape and Urban Planning. 80: 223–236.

Chapter 6: Management Implications

Robert Rainville

Introduction

This analysis was performed at a broad scale, incorporating three national forests—each consisting of several ranger districts. Forest conditions vary widely across this area. To evaluate the report's validity and utility and to identify management implications and needs, four national forest managers with extensive work experience on the Blue Mountains national forests were asked to review this report and share their insights.[1]

Results

The report's primary findings are valid. Restoration work is heavily reliant on management's ability to remove small-diameter trees. Challenges arise in treating this material owing to its low value and the high costs of removal.

The report verifies local land managers' observations that the land base to support timber harvest targets is in reality smaller than anticipated in past planning exercises. Restrictions and best management practices developed since forest plans were approved in the early 1990s have reduced the land base for harvest and mechanical restoration activities.

Prior to the report's release, managers, community leaders, and elected officials held a wide variety of views. Although there was general agreement on the significance of forest health conditions, there was limited understanding of the effect multiple-use management objectives had on thinning, and minimal appreciation of the financial realities that limit restorative treatments. After the report's release, local, community, state, and federal leaders have come to better agreement on the challenges facing the forests and communities in the Blue Mountains. Cooperation in finding solutions is now more likely.

> The report verifies local land managers' observations that the land base to support timber harvest targets is in reality smaller than anticipated in past planning exercises.

---

[1] The information in this chapter was provided during a September 26, 2005, conversation with:

- Jeff Blackwood, retired Forest Supervisor of the Umatilla National Forest
- Craig Smith-Dixon, Ranger on the North Fork John Day Ranger District
- Richard Haines, retired Ranger on the Whitman Unit (Baker, Pine, and Unity Ranger Districts) and the Prairie City Ranger District
- Kurt Wiedenmann, Ranger on the La Grande Ranger District

The author is a retired ranger and former director of the Blue Mountain Demonstration area.

Managers of the Blue Mountains national forests must overcome the financial limitations described in this analysis when trying to thin and restore densely stocked[2] stands. Stands where thinning operations can be accomplished with a positive net return are generally scattered and account for only 10 to 15 percent of the area being considered for treatment. On most densely stocked acres, the small volume of merchantable trees harvested with restoration prescriptions is inadequate to pay for the removal of small-diameter white fir (*Abies concolor* Gord. & Glend.) that is abundant in these stands.

Pursuit of multiple resource objectives also reduces the number of acres where thinning prescriptions should be applied. Some densely stocked stands are located in management areas where timber harvest or mechanical treatments are counter to forest plan direction. In areas where mechanical harvest could occur, densely stocked stands may not be treated because they provide important resource needs such as elk cover. The report's projections of treatable acres and commercially removable timber volumes are likely high because site-specific needs, such as bald eagle (*Haliaeetus leucocephalus* Linn.) nests, fragile viewsheds, special local places, and snag requirements were not considered. The report, therefore, represents an upper limit for possible timber harvest given current laws, regulations, and prevailing public opinion about how federally administered forests should be managed.

The requirement to maintain live trees greater than 21 inches diameter at breast height has a small effect on managers' ability to treat densely stocked stands. Large trees are generally lacking on the forests, especially in areas where mechanical treatments have been possible. Where large trees are found, they are often needed to meet multiple-use objectives that were not analyzed in the study. Unless there is some compelling ecological reason, their short supply makes it unlikely that managers would add larger trees to the harvest to make thinning operations financially feasible.

To implement restoration prescriptions in light of these limitations, managers must be strategic, collaborative, and in tune with changes in policies, technology, and markets. Most managers perform cursory analyses of drainage areas before committing staff time to planning particular projects. From this initial analysis, they evaluate resource conditions, management needs, financial limitations, and the degree of public support. To maximize use of their resources, managers select planning areas where the results of these initial analyses indicate that a restoration

> **To implement restoration prescriptions, managers must be strategic, collaborative, and in tune with changes in policies, technology, and markets.**

---

[2] Densely stocked stands are defined here as stands with stocking of greater than 45 percent of the maximum stand density index or more than 300 trees per acre smaller than 4 inches at breast height.

project would be environmentally and socially acceptable and financially viable. Although restoration treatments in controversial areas such as lynx (*Lynx canadensis* Kerr) habitat, riparian areas, and other special areas are legally permissible, they are generally avoided owing to budget and personnel limitations.

Most managers seek to work collaboratively with public groups throughout the planning process. With early involvement, public interests can be incorporated into the design of the project. Where good working relationships become established, the chance of last-minute surprises that can slow or prevent the project are reduced.

Changes in market conditions and technological advances can significantly affect economic conditions and therefore managers' ability to implement restoration treatments. Many densely stocked stands could be treated if markets for small trees improved or if transportation and processing of the harvested materials could be accomplished with less expense. A manager's awareness of changes in these conditions is important in planning activities that could be implemented.

Similarly, changes in agency policies and public laws significantly affect management options. Adoption of the policy that allows managers to reinvest proceeds from stand treatments that have positive net revenues into thinning treatments on stands where costs exceed receipts has been very beneficial. Most managers use this new stewardship authority to treat many more acres than otherwise would be possible.

The Healthy Forest Restoration Act (HFRA) of 2003 is an important piece of legislation that places an emphasis on treatment of fire-prone forests near urban areas. To be competitive for funding, Blue Mountain managers will need to adjust their fire hazard management programs to reflect the funding priority given to protection of wildland-urban interface. Management's historical reliance on larger scale analyses in identifying and evaluating project work must be modified owing to direction and funding associated with HFRA. Managers can avoid wasteful expenditures of resources and take advantage of opportunities by anticipating and aligning their programs with policy changes.

Challenges facing national forest managers in the Blues are difficult and call for long-term solutions. The following are ideas that would be beneficial:

1. Development of technologies that provide new markets for small trees, reducing impacts of mechanical treatments on the land, and reducing costs of transporting harvested material from forests to manufacturing facilities would allow managers to treat more densely stocked areas.

2. Incentives that make removal and industrial utilization of small trees financially feasible would encourage restoration treatments.

3. Analysis tools that allow decisionmakers to predict the long-term effectiveness of restoration activities would be helpful. Managers are capable of estimating short-term effects of individual actions, but have difficulty in predicting future risks and benefits arising from the cumulative effect of their activities. A scientifically credible tool that provides these estimates and displays results in an easily understandable way would be helpful in working with public groups and responding to legal challenges.

4. A scientific assessment of the effectiveness of restoration work that has been completed in specific watersheds would help managers. In watersheds such as Meadow Creek, where management has implemented several projects, how do resource conditions compare to conditions that would exist if management had not occurred? Answering this question would help managers assess what, if any, management is beneficial over time, and how their strategies may be improved.

5. Policies and budgets that allow evaluation of landscape-level resource needs and concerns associated with specific projects are needed. With passage of the HFRA, managers can speed project implementation by use of categorical exclusions (the lowest level environmental analysis allowed under the National Environmental Policy Act of 1969 and related regulations) for site-specific treatments. This new policy should be used in conjunction with larger scale evaluations of the proposed projects so that managers can consider issues and opportunities that are more apparent at a larger scale.

6. With 61 percent of the Blue Mountain national forests unavailable for mechanical treatment of densely stocked conditions, alternative management strategies for these areas would be beneficial. What restoration strategies could be used where some vegetation treatment is compatible with management objectives?

> **Cooperation is necessary between managers and scientists in developing practices to manage old-growth resources through time.**

7. A scientific analysis on how forest conditions have changed since the release of the vegetation report in 2002 would allow managers to assess the effects of policy changes.

8. Cooperation is necessary between managers and scientists in developing practices to manage old-growth resources through time. Presently, national forests have designated old-growth areas. This designation generally means that little management occurs in these stands. Is this the best policy? Could limited thinning help maintain old-growth attributes? How will replacement stands be designated and managed? Cooperation between

managers, communities, and scientists in developing management strategies that sustain old growth by providing a continuous supply of replacement stands would be more compatible with ecological conditions in the Blue Mountains than trying to preserve forever those that currently exist. Incentives to promote broader community representation and collaboration would be useful in sorting out an ecologically feasible and socially acceptable old-growth management policy.

9. Management policies that focus on ecological reestablishment of landscape balance rather than economic outcomes would benefit managers facing forest health concerns. Policies that emphasize what is left behind rather than what is removed are more appropriate in addressing issues that are bundled under the heading "forest health." Outcomes such as "resilience to natural and human-caused disturbances" would provide a better measure of success.

Chapter 7: Summary and Conclusions

Robert Rainville

A team of forest managers and scientists from Oregon State University, Oregon Department of Forestry, the Wallowa-Whitman, Malheur, and Umatilla National Forests, and the U.S. Department of Agriculture Forest Service Pacific Northwest Research Station prepared this assessment of the location, maximum volume, and composition of timber products that could result from a program designed to restore federally administered forests in the Blue Mountains of Oregon to conditions more similar to those that existed prior to Euro-American settlement. Such a restoration program would serve the dual purposes of (1) making these forests more resilient to natural and human-caused disturbances, and (2) stimulating economic activities that benefit the people who live in the Blue Mountains. This assessment included private, state, and federally administered lands within Baker, Grant, Harney, Morrow, Umatilla, Union, and Wallowa Counties of Oregon. Lands in Crook and Wheeler Counties managed by the Malheur National Forest were also analyzed. Forest management since 1988 was reviewed to provide an historical context for existing forest conditions.

The Forest Service administers 5,500,000 acres in the Blue Mountains of Oregon. Most of the land (3,884,000 acres or 71 percent) is not available for substantial and sustainable harvesting of timber. As a result of Congressional designations, forest planning allocations, or nonforested conditions, only minimal amounts of timber would be harvested during restoration treatments. Prescribed fire would be the primary tool available to accomplish fuel reduction and thinning (on many acres, fuel reduction could not be accomplished without first doing some mechanical treatment). Most of the wildfires that have occurred since 1988 have burned in these areas, a trend likely to continue.

The remaining 29 percent (1,616,000 acres) of land administered by the Forest Service available for substantial and sustainable timber harvest (referred to as active forestry lands in this report) has been actively managed over the last three decades. Up to 32 percent of this area has experienced timber harvest or noncommercial thinning since 1988.

Assessment results estimated that 943,000 acres of active forestry lands (58 percent) are densely stocked.[1] The approximate location of these stands is displayed in maps in this publication. Nearly half of these densely stocked acres (472,000) are not suitable for commercial thinning treatments, because they would yield only incidental amounts of merchantable timber (less than 400 cubic feet per acre) (fig. 7-1).

Assessment results estimated that 943,000 acres of active forestry lands are densely stocked. Nearly half of these acres are not suitable for commercial thinning

[2] Densely stocked stands are defined here as stands with stocking of greater than 45 percent of the maximum stand density index or more than 300 trees per acre smaller than 4 inches at breast height.

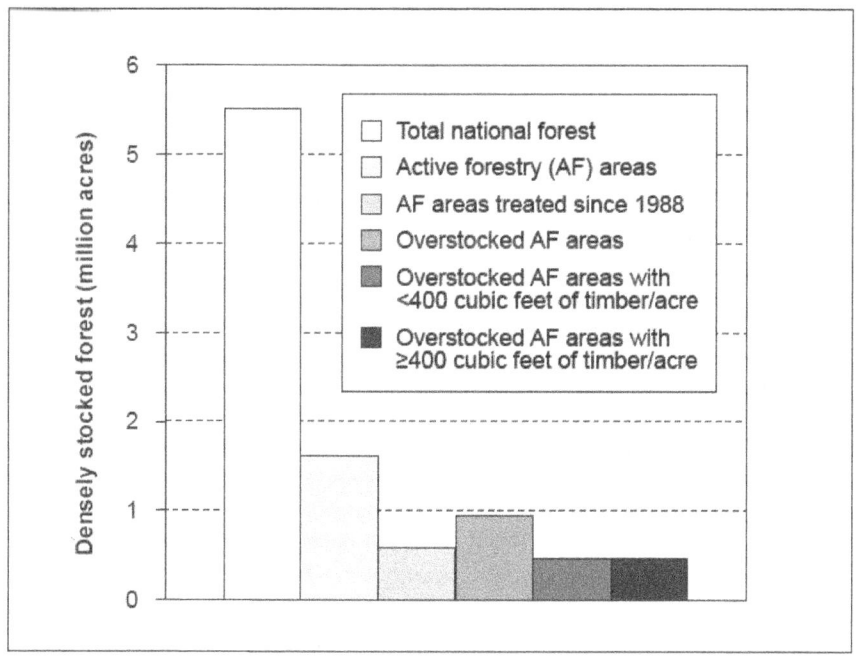

Figure 7-1—Potential for commercial thinning of densely stocked lands on national forests.

Commercial thinning of the remaining 471,000 acres would be difficult to accomplish economically. When a simulated thinning prescription was applied, most (66 percent) of the trees harvested were less than 13 inches diameter at breast height (d.b.h.), and the average quantity of timber removed was 3,200 board feet (BF)/acre. High operational costs and low market values associated with harvest of such low volumes of small trees would undermine the potential for commercial treatments on most densely stocked acres. Thinning on only 39,900 acres (± 4,600) was found to have a positive net revenue based upon the financial assumptions used in this analysis. These treatments would harvest 167 million BF (± 36). Douglas-fir (*Pseudotsuga menziesii* (Mirb.) Franco), grand fir (*Abies grandis* Dougl. ex D. Don), and ponderosa pine (*Pinus ponderosa* P. & C. Lawson) would account for 80 percent of the harvest.

Many of the densely stocked acres would have borderline commercial potential. Thinning of 136,000 acres could be accomplished with investments of less than $250 per acre. Another 138,000 acres could be thinned for $250 to $500 per acre.

Reductions in harvest and transportation costs, increased demand by industrial users of small wood, availability of subsidies, and/or modification of agency policies would be needed to make thinning commercially viable on many of these densely stocked acres. Even when considered under the most favorable of assumptions, most densely stocked stands would not be treatable without significant investment.

The effect of the Regional Forester's Forest Plan Amendment 2 restriction (commonly known as the east-side screens) on harvest of trees larger than 21 inches d.b.h. was analyzed. The amendment was adopted to preserve trees larger than 21 inches d.b.h. for forest resources such as wildlife. To preserve these trees, the simulated prescription selected smaller healthy trees of desired species for removal as needed to achieve the appropriate stand density. When the constraint was removed, the number of acres with a positive net value increased to 79,100 acres ($\pm 5,700$), which made 356 million board feet (± 57) of saw logs available for commercial harvest. When the prescription was allowed to harvest greater than 21-inch d.b.h. trees if their species was not desired on the site or if they were damaged or diseased, a 64-percent increase in the harvest of trees larger than 16 inches d.b.h. (from 456 to 750 BF per acre) was observed. Because harvest of larger trees is more efficient and results in greater volumes per acre, thinning on an additional 39,200 acres had a positive net value.

This simulation's estimate of the effect of the 21-inch d.b.h. restriction is likely an overestimate. During planning of thinning operations, localized requirements of large-tree-dependent resources would be considered. These management needs could result in significant reductions in the acres and timber volumes estimated in this assessment. Estimates reported here should be considered upper limits unless laws, regulations, or management policies for federally administered lands change.

The assessment found that 114,900 acres could be thinned and 392 million board feet (MMBF) of saw logs could be harvested commercially, if national forests were able to reinvest receipts from the thinning of stands with positive net values to treat those with negative net values. When reinvestment of receipts was combined with elimination of the restriction on harvest of trees larger than 21 inches d.b.h., the number of acres that could be treated increased to 223,100 yielding 807 MMBF of saw logs.

There are 1,161,000 acres of private forest lands in the Blue Mountains. State, county, and Bureau of Land Management forest lands total about 90,000 acres. The Oregon Department of Forestry estimates that 581,000 acres (50 percent) of the private forest lands are densely stocked. Ongoing analysis will estimate volume, size, species composition, and commercial value of timber products resulting from thinning these lands.

This analysis provides a landscape-level overview of management needs, opportunities, and challenges associated with restoration of densely stocked forests within the Blue Mountains. Although individual county results are reported, reliability of the more localized estimates is subject to the following analysis limitations:

- Only a small number of sample plots were available in some counties. In these situations, the limited sample size may not accurately represent overall county conditions. Ninety-five-percent confidence limits are provided to display the relative reliability of the data.

- Management concerns such as cumulative effects on wildlife and aquatic resources, soil and visual sensitivity, and operational feasibility could not be assessed at this scale. As a result, this report's estimates of acres available for treatment and quantities of timber resulting from thinning likely exceed attainable levels.

- The analysis is based upon application of a simulated thinning prescription and regional economic data. Changes in the prescription and economic assumptions to account for local vegetation management needs, operational capabilities, and markets would alter the results.

- The economic assessment only considered expenses associated with thinning of merchantable trees. Costs to treat nonmerchantable material that is contributing to forest health risks were not included.

Metric Equivalents

When you know:	Multiply by:	To find:
Feet	0.305	Meters
Acres	.405	Hectares
Million board feet (MMBF)	5.67	Thousand cubic meters
Cubic feet	.0283	Cubic meters
Cubic feet per acre	.0699	Cubic meters per hectare
Board feet (BF)	.0024	Cubic meters
Board feet per acre	.014	Cubic meters per hectare